T0195696

Also by Ryan Andrew Smith

Not That God:

Trading the Believable Lie for the Unbelievable Truth

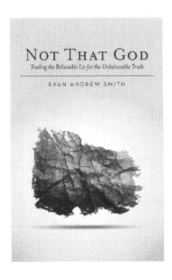

Do you ever have trouble reconciling the goodness of God with the waiting, doubt, tension, and tragedy you see in the world? Does the voice of doubt ever whisper, "What on earth is God doing?"

Gospel-centered and biblically saturated, *Not That God* discusses weighty themes in an honest, approachable, and conversational way. Through the lens of John 11 (The Death of Lazarus), Ryan helps us see how God is glorified even in the most unexpected of circumstances.

If you have ever had a question about God, wrestled with an aspect of His sovereignty, or simply think you already know all there is to know about God, you may be greatly helped by this book.

TRUST THE CIRCLE

*Understanding God's Design for
Sex, Gender, and Sexuality*

RYAN ANDREW SMITH

WESTBOW
PRESS®
A DIVISION OF THOMAS NELSON
& ZONDERVAN

WestBow Press books may be ordered through booksellers or by contacting:

WestBow Press
A Division of Thomas Nelson & Zondervan
1663 Liberty Drive
Bloomington, IN 47403
www.westbowpress.com
844-714-3454

Interior Image Credit: Ryan Andrew Smith

ISBN: 978-1-6642-7922-3 (sc)
ISBN: 978-1-6642-7921-6 (e)

Library of Congress Control Number: 2022917868

Print information available on the last page.

WestBow Press rev. date: 10/11/2022

To my amazing wife, Allison, and our
wonderful children, Kelen and London.
You are continual signs of God's love, grace, and mercy to me.

To my mom and dad.
Thank you for your continual encouragement and support.

To my beloved church family.
Thank you for walking the road of trusting
Jesus Christ together with me.

To all those struggling to understand their
place in God's story of sex and sexuality.
My prayers are with you as you read this book.
May God illuminate His path for you.

Ultimately, to God my Father, Creator,
Sustainer, Savior, and Friend.
May this be used in Your hands for Your
glory among Your people.

It would seem that our Lord finds our
desires not too strong, but too weak.
We are half-hearted creatures, fooling about with drink
and sex and ambition when infinite joy is offered us, like
an ignorant child who wants to go on making mud pies
in a slum because he cannot imagine what is meant by the
offer of a holiday at the sea. We are far too easily pleased.[1]

—C. S. Lewis, *The Weight of Glory*

[1]   C. S. Lewis, *The Weight of Glory: And Other Addresses,* (New York: Macmillan, 1949), 26.

CONTENTS

PART 1
Introduction

What Is This Book?

This is a book about sex.

This is also a book about gender, marriage, sexuality, and a host of other things.

More than any of those things, however, this is a book about God.

The truth is either there is a God or there isn't. This God has either created us, our world, and everything in it or He hasn't. If He has created, either He is personal and involved with His creation or He isn't. If He is personal with us, it would only make sense that He communicates with us. But is there a God, has He created, is He personal, and has He spoken to us?

The Bible and the person of Jesus answer all those questions with a resounding *yes*! God is there. He has created. Not only is He personal, but also He has spoken with us and given Himself to us that we might understand His creation, His character, His provision, His goodness, His glory, and what it means to follow a perfect God in a broken world.

If God has spoken to us, it means He cares about us. It means that in a world where we often seem confused and are looking for what is true, God knows the path that is true, and He wants us to follow Him on it for our good. It also means there are dangers to be avoided outside of God's path that we may not perceive, understand, or even consider dangerous.

I don't know why you're reading this book, but I want you to know why I wrote it. I didn't write it because I wanted to write a book about sex. You're probably not reading this because you wanted to read a book about sex either. I wrote this book because I believe God is real, and I love Jesus. I trust Him. As I've tried to trust and follow Jesus in my life, I have often failed. I have also seen the natural consequences of that failure and don't want to repeat those mistakes, though I often do.

While veering from God's good and expressed path, we might feel good, excited, even "right." Something within us cries out for the adventure of forging our own path, writing our own story, and making our own destiny. When we walk away from God or deny His very existence, it can easily seem like we are on the edge of something new—something exciting—a path that leads away from what is known. To be honest, the path away from God is not new and exciting; it's actually very old, well-worn, tried, and has been found lacking.

In today's culture, the path away from God is the well-lit path, and it may seem that everyone is on it. It's the inviting path, and there are many who encourage you to walk it. But is it the right path? Is it true? Does it actually lead to flourishing, joy, peace, and ultimate love? Is it *good*?

I'm writing this book to call from a different path. In fact, while the path I'm calling you to may not be well lit in today's society, it is well worn by the feet of those who have trusted and followed it in all of life for the rest of life. It's a path as old as time yet more relevant today than you can imagine. The voices that call to it may be quieter, but I want you to listen for them. They celebrate and agree with the voice of Jesus in the book of John when He says, "I am the way, and the truth, and the life. No one comes to the Father [God] except through me" (John 14:6 ESV).

What does this have to do with sex and sexuality? Quite a bit, actually. Could it be that God has woven truth, beauty, love, and even the great story of His redeeming a broken people into the very fibers of sex and sexuality? What if God has given sex and sexuality not as subjective toys for us to use as we like but as intricately designed tools to be used in the grand narrative of God's story for all His creation. What if you've been given a part in this great story? If so, it would seem important that we talk about it.

My goal in writing this book is that you would be equipped with the truth that a very good God has given us very good gifts in sex and sexuality. Like any tools of importance, we need to make sure we are asking the right questions about them. What are they for? What do they make? Are there dangers if we use them the wrong way?

If you are someone who has grown up in church and is wanting to trust and follow Jesus, it's likely that you know about sex but haven't heard a lot taught about it from the Bible. My hope in writing this is that you will see that the Bible has a *lot* to say about sex and sexuality, and it's actually really good. If you haven't grown up around church and conversations about God and "the gospel," you may be hesitant to read this book. You may be cautious or somewhat guarded as you approach these ideas. That's OK. I probably would be too.

For the Christian and non-Christian, I want you to feel safe reading this book. Ultimately, this is a book about what God is *for*, not just what He is against. God is calling all of us to embrace sex and sexuality in a way that seems countercultural but provides a path to true sexual freedom.

For Christians, I want to open the floodgates of this conversation for you and your church. For those who are wondering how to navigate our sex-saturated culture, I hope to give you a resource to explain to those around you what the Bible actually says about sex, gender, and sexuality. For the skeptic, atheist, or person who just isn't sure what's out there, I want you to have clear definitions of what the Bible says regarding sex, gender, and sexuality. You may be completely against what the Bible says and think that I'm a fool for believing it. That's fine. I just want you to know fully what the Bible says about sexuality and what I—and millions of others throughout history—actually believe.

To those of you who experience same-sex attraction, gender dysphoria, or have a checkered past with sex and sexuality, I want to first say that I am here to encourage you, not condemn you. I am not afraid of anyone or anti-anyone. I'm not here looking down on anyone. If you finish this book thinking that God and His people do not love you and want what's best for you, I have not accurately represented God or His people. If you come away from this book believing that you deserve to be treated any differently than the rest of us at the foot of the cross, I have not done my job and have missed my aim. I am sorry for my inability to represent God to you clearly through my words. Please forgive me. Whoever you are and whatever your background, I want you to know there is a God who made you, loves you, and is calling you to trust and follow Him in all your life, including your sexuality.

This book is not written to address one certain issue pertaining to conversations over sex and sexuality. Rather than chase side arguments or issues of the day, this book is written to focus on what God has made clear, not what seems fuzzy to us on the edges. In fact, what I hope you see as you read this book is that God has clearly defined for us what is right, true, and good in relation to sex and sexuality. He has so clearly defined it that we can draw a circle of sorts detailing what is inside and outside God's good and protective plan for human flourishing. Throughout this book, we will refer to that clear boundary as "the circle" of God's protection, provision, and design.

This book is written to invite you to trust that circle.

Thanks for reading.

QUESTIONS FOR FURTHER STUDY AND REFLECTION

1. Why are you reading this book?
2. What do you expect this book to say about sex, gender, and sexuality?
3. What would someone who believes differently than you about God expect to find in this book? Why might they read it?
4. How much were you taught about sex growing up?

PART 2

THE RIGHT GOAL

The Winning Shot

I reached my peak of athletic accomplishment in elementary school. In fifth grade, I was the starting point guard for the Woodlands Eagles in our city league. Toward the end of the season, we found ourselves in a game competing neck and neck with the best team in the league. The team we were against was made of giants. They were all shaving in fifth grade. These guys threw backward alley-oops like free throws, and unlike me, they were only beginning what would undoubtedly be high-profile NBA careers.

OK, none of that is true. The fact that we were competitive in a game was a miracle in and of itself, but the fact that it was a game against such intimidating rivals made this the game we knew we would brag about to our future sons. With only a few seconds left in the game, we were ahead by two points. The team of giants scored a lay-up to tie the score. My teammate took the ball out of bounds, preparing to throw it in and drain the clock. Players from both teams were huddled in a mass of sweaty, stinky fifth-grade elbows and knees jockeying for position around mid-court to receive the lobbed throw. My teammate threw the ball into the tornadic mass of preteens, and whether by accident or divine sovereignty, though I was, by far, the shortest and least-skilled person on the court, the ball landed in my hands.

Glancing at the red digits of the game clock, I recognized that my destiny was coming into view. Five seconds. I had five seconds to run the length of half the court and lay in the basket for a win. No one stood in my way. Everything in the peripheral went dark, and all sounds faded to echoes as my heart began to pulsate through my chest. I ran toward the basket, dribbling with conscious precision. There was nothing on my mind but that basket and the years of untold glory that would enshrine our young team of warriors into the annals of history.

As I began my stride for the final shot, I could hear the crowd and my teammates yelling my name. They were going crazy. As the clock struck one second, I elevated and perfectly projected the ball toward the basket for a textbook layup. The swish of the net rang out along with the buzzer on the game clock, and I turned around to receive my teammates who were, no doubt, ready to congratulate me in an erupting dogpile of victory.

Instead, when I turned around, what I found was a confused mass of fifth-graders still standing at center court. Silent fans stood staring in disbelief with mouths open. As the ball slowly descended back to the court, I realized something was off. The court was turned around. Or as I slowly came to realize, in the chaos at center court vying for possession of the incoming lob, I had gotten turned around and caught the ball while facing the other team's basket. Instead of sealing what would have been the greatest basketball victory of the twentieth century for the Woodlands Eagles, I had mistakenly run toward the wrong goal, scored, and won the game for the other team.

I tell you that story to tell you the important lesson I learned that day, which I have carried with me throughout my entire life: *Intention is only as good as direction.* If the goal is wrong, then how you pursue it doesn't matter. You can have all the right intention, desire, skill, and execution, but if the goal is wrong, none of those things make a difference.

When it comes to talking about sex and sexuality, most of the conversation and emphasis in our culture and the church has been on the pursuit, the *how*, and not the goal, the *what*. We have focused on *how* to pursue (or not pursue) sex and not on *what* it is we are pursuing. Our society champions the pursuit of sex and sexuality as guided by personal feelings. The mantra of our day is "What I feel determines what I want, and the fulfillment of that desire is what is most important." In that case, what is "right" is simply being true to yourself, however you define that.

In the church, for a long time, the goal has been just to keep kids from having sex. The mantra for Christians for decades has just been "Don't." *Don't look at porn because nakedness is bad. Don't ever have sex because you'll get an STD. Sex hurts, you'll be damaged goods, and sex is gross. If you do, God will be mad at you, you'll have no place in the church, and your only choice is to keep quiet or go to reparative therapy.* In many ways, that has often been the church's approach to sexual purity.

The issue with those approaches is that neither of them are what the Bible teaches about sex and sexuality. When it comes to sex and sexuality, many voices around us have championed an all-or-nothing approach. Either sex is a god or sex is the devil. The Bible, however, says that something is right only as long as it is true, and there is a truth about sex and sexuality.

Any discussion on how we should direct our sex and sexuality must first focus on the question "What is true?" In other words, what is the right goal? Is the goal simply up to us individually to define, or has it been defined for us? Can we run to any basket we choose and call it right, or is there such a thing as a right basket?

As we walk together through the next few pages, my aim is to show from the Scriptures that God has clearly defined what sex, gender, and sexuality are. He has told us what is true. In doing so, God calls us to pursue sex and sexuality rightly for our good, our joy, and ultimately, His glory.

What If …

What if I told you that sex is not ultimately about you?

What if I told you that sex is not ultimately about your partner?

What if I told you that your gender is not ultimately about you?

What if I told you that sex, gender, and sexuality are actually about a much greater and bigger story than you could ever imagine? What if I told you that regardless of who you are, you have a part to play in that story?

The purpose of this book is not to argue but to inform. There are many ideas about what sexuality is and how it should be used. You may have learned your ideas about sex and sexuality from parents, friends, the media, or personal experience. One question you may have wondered is, *Why are Christians so weird about sex, gender, and sexuality?*

The truth is that everyone, including you and me, has a worldview. A worldview is a lens that shapes how we see the world and our experiences, including how we understand sex, gender, and sexuality. We have learned and formed our worldviews regarding sex and other related topics largely based on what has been modeled or explained to us. Often our worldviews are formed by what people we admire uphold as right. Sometimes our worldviews are formed in reaction to the views of certain people we don't admire or don't want to be like.

For Christians, the Bible is meant to be our ultimate worldview-shaper. Christ followers believe that the Bible is the Word of God. The Bible tells us everything we need to know about God, ourselves, and how to live. One of the many things the Bible talks about is sexuality. In fact, the Bible talks more about sex, gender, and sexuality than you might think. The reason the Bible talks so much about sex, gender, and sexuality is that God says sex is good. God created gender. God made sexuality, and He talks a lot about it in His Word. The reason God talks so much about sexuality is that, ultimately, sex, gender, and sexuality tell a much greater story than just our attraction and physical pleasure.

What Is Love?

The popular saying "Love is love" may sound true on some level, but what is love? The topic of love is very familiar yet not necessarily well understood. Love is incredibly simple yet infinitely complex. In the Bible, God says that He is love (1 John 4:8 ESV). As we mentioned earlier, Jesus says that He is also the way, the *truth*, and the life. Often, in our world, it seems as though we are faced with the options of God's truth *or* His love as if they are two mutually exclusive options. We may ask whether we should love a person *or* tell them the truth.

What God tells us openly and unapologetically in His Word is that God's *truth*—what is revealed in His Word—is *one* with His *love*. Love and truth are not two distinct options. Rather, when applied rightly, truth and love are one option and truly the only option for anyone who desires to find joy, purpose, and fulfillment. God's love is central to His truth. His way is the loving way. His life is a life of true love.

Unfortunately, love is a topic that in our day and age has been reduced to being fully synonymous with sex itself. I don't necessarily blame our culture for this, it's simply how many of our worldviews have been formed by the information available to us. We may have never heard about God's love expressed in His design for sex and sexuality. The truth is that the church's voice as a whole has been very silent on gender and sexual issues. Therefore, the assumption has been made that God doesn't know much about sex, He doesn't care, or He doesn't want to talk about it. It's as if He just made it, threw it to the side, and said, "Yuck! You all figure it out." Either way, the Bible, God, and the church are often not seen as resources for developing the right worldview regarding sexuality.

The problem with that is the Bible itself.

The truth is that the Bible is very explicit about what sex and gender are. It actually celebrates those things. The Bible also talks about the joyful yet difficult pursuit of right sexual relations, ways to enjoy God's gift of sex, and pitfalls to avoid in trying to navigate a sexual and gender-conscious world. The topics are prominent in virtually every book of the Bible yet hushed in many of our pulpits.

The Bible has a lot to say about sex and sexuality. God has clearly defined what sex and sexuality are. God made gender. God made marriage. God made sex. He didn't create them for us to be confused or quiet about them.

QUESTIONS FOR FURTHER STUDY AND REFLECTION

1. What is something you learned from this chapter?
2. Where have you learned your ideas about sex and sexuality (media, friends, family, etc.)?
3. How would you define "love"?
4. How does your definition of "love" relate to the reality of truth?
5. How do you think God views sex and sexuality? Why do you think that?

PART 3
WHAT IS BIBLICAL GENDER?

First Things First

> *In the beginning, God created the heavens and the earth.*
> —Genesis 1:1 ESV

Genesis 1:1 contains the very first words in all of the Bible. The very first thing we are told about life, God, ourselves, the world, the supernatural, and everything in existence is that in the beginning, God created the heavens and the earth. Why is this important? It's important because these words explain to us, first and foremost, that everything is *by* God, everything is *for* God, and God is the sovereign King over everything. Our God is actively involved in His creation because all creation is His.

Genesis 1 also shows us that God is a God of order, design, and purpose. As we read the rest of the opening chapter of Genesis, we see that God defines, creates, and then separates everything. God is a God of order. God defines, creates, and then separates land and water. He defines, creates, and then separates light from dark. He defines, creates, and then separates day from night, etc., and gives each creation a distinct harmonious purpose.

Toward the end of the first chapter of Genesis, we read in verses 27–28, "So God created [humankind] in His own image, in the image of God He created them; male and female He created them. God blessed them; and God said to them, 'Be fruitful and increase in number; fill the earth and subdue it'" (Genesis 1:27–28 NIV).

What we see in these verses is that God defines and creates yet another distinction: humans from animals and everything else. The purpose of this creation and distinction, we are told, is to image, represent, and display God. The image of God is often referred to as the *Imago Dei*. In the opening chapter of the Bible, in a few simple verses, God gives us the ultimate *what* and *why* for humanity.

Notice, the first things we learn about human beings created as image-bearers in God's likeness are in relation to their gender and sexuality. God created humans. He created them male and female. He told them to be fruitful and multiply—have sex and have babies. Genesis 1 tells us that in the beginning, among other beautiful creations of order, design, and purpose, God created gender, sex, and sexuality.

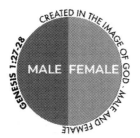

OTHER CREATION

Are Genders Different?

Ten years ago, the question of whether or not genders are different likely would not have needed to be asked. The idea that genders are distinct has been a base-level, cross-cultural understanding, and observation among people since the beginning of time. However, today those who make this same statement in the public square do so with a degree of fear or anxiety. This topic makes a lot of noise. At the heart of this discussion is the question of whether genders are just cultural constructs that must be taken apart for the sake of social progression. Isn't gender distinctiveness outdated? Can't we just leave the idea of a gender binary behind?

The Bible tells its readers that genders have certain traits and unchangeable realities that not only make them separate, but also useful for God's glory and our good. As we saw previously, in the opening chapter of Genesis, God created the dividing line between male and female genders on purpose. The first thing God says in the Bible about humans is that they are made in the image of God as a complementary pair, meaning they are different, but they go together. There can be no humankind without their existence as male and female.

God's creation of people in Genesis 1 concludes an amazing unfolding account in which God creates light, water, earth, vegetation, and living creatures. These creatures, created according to their "kinds," are created to reproduce with others of their kind. God tells them, "Be fruitful and multiply and fill the waters of the seas, and let birds multiply on the earth" (Genesis 1:22 ESV).

While God gives the same command to humans in verse 28 of chapter 1, something is different between humans and the rest of God's creation. Genesis 2:18, 22 record, "Then the Lord God said, 'It is not good for the man to be alone; I will make him a helper suitable for him …' The man gave names to all the cattle, and to the birds of the sky, and to every beast of the field, but for Adam there was not found a helper suitable for him" (Genesis 2:18, 22 NASB). Yet when God makes Eve and brings her to Adam, Adam says, "This is now bone of my bones, and flesh of my flesh; she shall be called Woman because she was taken out of Man" (Genesis 2:23 NASB).

Eve was the same as Adam in a way the animals were not. Adam and Eve were of the same "kind." They shared a form and function in a way that only humans can. As a different and higher kind than the animals, God gave humans a different and higher responsibility. God made humankind distinct with a certain purpose.

If these verses ended the entire creation account, we might think that humans were just some kind of alpha animal like a lion prowling the Serengeti or a great white shark lurking the Australian reefs. Yet the Bible purposely highlights something unique about God's creation of humans and His command for them to reproduce. The Bible says God has made humans male and female in His very image.

Before the creation of man, God created animals on the earth and divided them into distinct sexes, which made the natural processes possible that would allow them to reproduce and fulfill the purpose God had given them. In other words, He created them to have sex and have babies. But the Bible doesn't highlight the fact that animals were created male and female in the same way it does when God creates humans, even though animals certainly were male and female. Even though animals were made male and female, the fact that the Bible says human beings were made male and female is important. People are separated into binary male and female, which means certain important things related to their being made in the image of God. The Bible says distinct human genders do not exist just for reproduction or sexual fulfillment. As Victor Hamilton explains, "Sexuality is not an accident of nature, nor is it simply a biological phenomenon. Instead, it is a gift of God."[2]

In these verses from Genesis, we see that humanity is created with sameness and difference. "Humankind," originally written in Hebrew as the word *adam*, in Genesis 1:27, fulfills the God-ordained purpose of being made in God's image. This idea is immediately reaffirmed in the biblical text as the author states, "In the image of God He created them."

And who is the "them"? Immediately following this, the author identifies who exactly makes up the plural category of *adam* or "humankind": "Male and female He created them" (Genesis 1:27 ESV).

In other words, God made people. People are important because they are created with the image of God stamped on them. People are males or females yet carry the *Imago Dei*. Males are not females, nor are females males. They are different—separate. Yet males and females are the same in that they are stamped with the image of God.

It is important that we understand that males and females are the same in their status as God's image-bearers. Both sexes mirror God physically, relationally, emotionally, and in a variety

---

[2] Victor Hamilton, *The Book of Genesis, Chapters 1–17* (Grand Rapids: Eerdman's, 1990), 138.

of other ways. Males and females image God together in sameness *and* separately through their differences. Created in this way, God tells men and women together to have dominion over the earth in Genesis 1:29.

As man and woman, they share the honor of being God's image-bearers. God calls them to obedience to Him, which again shows their equality. They are called together to image God as they trust Him, follow Him, uphold His design, and walk in His ways. Men and women are created as equals in responsibility and ability to display the image of God as binary males and females.

This unity of the two, male and female, under the one banner of "humankind" isn't just a big fancy idea or something that exists only in philosophy. The fact that men and women are separate yet belong together is also pragmatic; meaning, they are designed with purpose to function a certain way. Though distinct, God created male and female genders to be unbreakably linked. Men need women, and women need men. Each gender needs the other gender to be different from them in the way they function but the same in the way they're formed. God created two genders: male and female. These two genders were meant to be together.

While the opening chapter of Genesis is very specific in its statement that the two genders are the same in value, there is an important difference between them as well. The Old Testament was originally written in the Hebrew language. When our English translation of the Bible says, "*suitable* for him" in Genesis 2:18, it is a translation of the Hebrew word *neged*.[3] This word in Hebrew more fully means "opposite" or "counterpart." The word also means "corresponding," "in front of," and "opposite in position of," sort of like two puzzle pieces placed next to each other.

---

[3]   William L. Holladay, Walter Baumgartner, and Ludwig Köhler. *A Concise Hebrew and Aramaic Lexicon of the Old Testament.* (Grand Rapids: Eerdman's, 1989), 226.

Not only are male and female human beings made as the same kind, just like two different puzzle pieces are made as the same kind, but they are also made with important differences like puzzle pieces (we will pick up on this more later). We see these differences highlighted after the man and woman rebel against God in Genesis 3 (often called "the fall"). After the fall in Genesis 3, though man and woman received the same consequences for fighting against God's goodness and authority over them, these consequences were applied differently. The woman would have increased pain in childbearing, and the man would have pain and toil as he worked the ground. Both were equally fallen and had equal consequences, yet God still went to the man first as the one who held primary responsibility for the couple. Even though they were completely equal in substance and value, they were given different roles or functions. What this means is that even though men and women are created the same in value, they are different in the ways they apply that value. Men and women need the differences found in each other to fully function as humanity.

God divided male and female into two different genders not in spite of their sameness but as a wonderful and beautiful expression of it. God has woven the binary separation of genders into the very fabric of our physical being. In fact, there are over 6,500 genetic differences between males and females that we know of. These differences don't exist on a spectrum but are either one or the other, either male or female. Each person is born with two chromosomes. Either those chromosomes are an XY pair or they are an XX pair. If XY, the person has those 6,500 distinct physical traits that make him male. If chromosomes are XX, they have the 6,500 distinct physical traits that make her female. While the physical part of us isn't the only part of us, it lies at the very center of who we are as a person. These realities do not and cannot change. While there may be a big difference in the way our personalities or likes and dislikes are shown in us, they are always shown in the context of our being male or female.

Far from being restrictive, the Bible says that our binary gender distinction is something to be excited about. The Bible celebrates diversity expressed by the two genders. Our culture says that if you have a combination of "feminine" and "masculine" traits, you aren't really a man or a woman but exist on a spectrum that slides between the two. Using very strict gender stereotypes, our culture says that any move away from what is culturally expressed as a "man's man" or a "girly girl" separates you from your gender. That idea couldn't be further from the truth.

Rather than saying a man who likes art or dance isn't a man, the Bible celebrates male art-makers and dancers as wonderful expressions of the male gender. Rather than saying a woman who likes sports isn't a woman, the Bible celebrates strong women who express their femininity in a variety of ways.

Do you know who is the first person in the Bible mentioned as being filled with the Spirit of God? It's a man named Bezalel. Who was Bezalel? Was he a strong warrior or a mighty king? No, Bezalel was an artist and craft-maker. In Exodus 31:3–5 God says, "I have filled him with the Spirit of God, with ability and intelligence, with knowledge, and all craftsmanship, to devise artistic designs, to work in gold, in silver, and in bronze, in cutting stones for setting, and in carving wood, to work in every craft" (ESV).

The passage goes on to explain that God has filled Bezalel with the Spirit to make clothes, anointing oils, and fragrant perfumes. Because of his work and passions, Bezalel would not be considered manly by today's standards. In God's eyes, however, Bezalel was a strong and courageous man who expressed his God-given masculinity through art and craft.

Deborah was a leading judge in Israel. Lydia was a successful businesswoman who was instrumental in the life of the church at Philippi. A woman named Jael jammed a tent peg through the skull of a bad guy who ran by her tent. These women and many others in the Bible would be told today that they are expressing masculine traits outside of womanhood. The Bible says that those traits are beautiful, strong, confident expressions of their God-given femininity.

The Bible is full of men who were poets, singers, and songwriters. Adam, David, Solomon, Moses, Joshua, Asaph, Jehoshaphat, Isaiah, Ezekiel, Amos, Habakkuk, Jeremiah, and many other men have songs or poems recorded in the Scripture. Jesus and His disciples sang together. When the apostle Paul found himself in a dangerous and life-threatening situation, he turned immediately to song. The Bible is a champion of diversity within gender. The church should be as well.

The Bible says that there are two genders: male and female. The Bible also says that these two genders are filled with colorful, amazing, broad, unique, and necessary expressions of masculinity and femininity. Genders are different, and that's *a beautiful thing.*

Genders Reunited

The creation story of Genesis 1 could be summarized in the following way: God creates, God divides, and God purposes. God said, "Let there be light" (Genesis 1:3 ESV), and there was light. God separated the light from the darkness (1:4). God made and separated water from earth (1:6), organized plants by different kinds (1:11), and even made different lights in space to separate the day from the night (1:14). God not only separates things, but God also gives them purpose. Regarding these lights, God says, "Let them be for signs and for seasons, and for days and years, and let them be lights in the expanse of the heavens to give light upon the earth. And it was so" (Genesis 1:14–15 ESV).

God creates. God divides. God purposes.

Interestingly, as God creates, separates, and defines all His creation according to unique purposes, there is only one thing

God creates, separates, defines, then reunites. The opening pages of Genesis tell their readers that God not only created gender binary differences but that He also made those differences coexist in beautiful harmony. Even more than that, God created men and women to reunite in a certain way. This certain way is what the Bible calls "marriage."

QUESTIONS FOR FURTHER STUDY AND REFLECTION

1. What is something you learned from this chapter?
2. What significance does Genesis 1:1 have for us today?
3. Where have you developed your understanding of gender?
4. What are some different modern thoughts people have about gender? How do those thoughts compare to what we find in Genesis 1?
5. How are you going to apply what you learned in this chapter?

PART 4

WHAT IS BIBLICAL MARRIAGE?

A Controversial Statement

Here is a controversial statement in today's culture that I want to unpack throughout the rest of this chapter:

> God designed marriage as the covenant relationship between one man and one woman in all of life for the rest of life.

Why is that statement so controversial? Perhaps it is because the statement seems exclusive since it doesn't account for homosexual marriage. Perhaps the idea of marriage as a "covenant" seems outdated and restrictive. After all, aren't self-proclaimed Christians hypocritical since they have the same rate of divorce as those who don't profess to be Christians? Hasn't divorce become so common that we don't need to think of marriage as a covenant?

Those objections are valid. You might even have more objections to the statement. Does the Bible really say that God designed marriage as the covenant relationship between one man and one woman in all of life for the rest of life? If so, is that even a good thing?

God Designed Marriage …

Genesis 2 takes a closer look at God's creation process that was shown to us in Genesis 1. We can think of Genesis 1 and 2 as complementary far and near views. If Genesis 1 is a flyover of a forest, Genesis 2 is a walk on the ground through the trees.

Genesis 2:22–24 describes the very first coming together of the sexes. The account is considered by most Bible scholars to be the first marriage ceremony. The text says,

> And the rib that the Lord God had taken from the man He made into a woman and brought her to the man. Then the man said, "This at last is bone of my bones and flesh of my flesh; she shall be called Woman, because she was taken out of Man." Therefore a man shall leave his father and his mother and hold fast to his wife, and they shall become one flesh (Genesis 2:22–24 ESV).

When we look at these verses, we immediately see a few things. First, just as God created the heavens and the earth, God initiated, defined, and created what is called "marriage." Marriage was God's idea. Marriage belongs to God. God created marriage to be the covenant relationship between one man and one woman in all of life for the rest of life. God didn't create two women for Adam. God didn't create another man for Adam. God didn't even base His marital design on Adam and Eve's sexual attraction.

Because God joined Adam and Eve at the beginning of human time, throughout all time, culture, and history, a man is supposed to unite with *his* wife in the building of a new home, and the two shall become one flesh. Regarding these words in Genesis 2, Bible scholar Wayne Grudem says, "This standard for marriage should apply to all people, not merely to Christians or those who personally happen to agree with the Bible's standards."[4]

What Grudem is saying is that this first marriage is an overarching principle that is built into the fabric of marriage itself. God gave and ordained marriage not to be a cultural expression of love or merely a social commitment but to be a covenantal standard throughout all societies and all ages.

How do we know this? As the author of Genesis, likely Moses, is describing the first marriage ceremony, he steps into the story to explain what is really going on in this marital union between Adam and Eve. The author says in Genesis 2:24, "Therefore a man shall leave *his* father and *his* mother and hold fast to *his* wife, and *they* shall become one flesh" (ESV, italics added). What God does with Adam and Eve is a pattern to be copied by all future marriage relationships.

God is being clear in His Word: Marriage is given and ordained by God alone. As Grudem notes, "When a marriage occurs, it is not merely a human ceremony. Rather, something deeply spiritual happens. God Himself joins the couple together in a spiritual union as husband and wife—their union is something that 'God has joined together.'"[5]

As the Covenant Relationship …

What do we mean by the word "covenant"? Christopher Yuan explains that a marital covenant is "a permanent, exclusive, and holistic union of two people."[6]

---

[4]   Wayne Grudem, *Christian Ethics: An Introduction to Biblical Moral Reasoning* (Wheaton: Crossway, 2018), 711.

[5]   Gordon J. Wenham, *Genesis 1–15* (Nashville: Thomas Nelson, 1987), 70.

[6]   Ibid., 88.

A covenant is a promise that is meant to be unbreakable. Marriage, as a covenant commitment, carries a lot of biblical weight and significance. God is a covenant-making God. Yuan relates, "God named Abraham and Israel when he entered into a covenant with each of them (Genesis 17:5; 35:10). In a similar manner, in Eden, the man named the woman when he entered into the covenant of marriage with her."[7]

Covenants bond two people so much that a new reality—a new name—is given. This is why when a man and woman get married, the wife usually takes on the last name of her husband. They are renamed in unity with each other because they are united in covenant with each other.

God is a covenantal God. This means that God is a God who makes and keeps His promises. Throughout the Scriptures, covenant language is used to describe the relationship between God and His people. The Hebrew word *āzab* (to leave or forsake) is often used by God to describe Israel's rejection of its covenantal vows and relationship with God. Likewise, the Hebrew word *dābaq* (to cling or be joined to) is often used in the Bible to describe the right keeping of the covenant relationship between God and His people. These are the same Hebrew words used in Genesis 2:24 to describe the husband and wife's relationship with each other. From the beginning and throughout the rest of the Bible, God shows us that marriage is meant to be more than just a declaration of love. Marriage is meant to be a promise made and a promise kept. The importance of this promise goes far beyond the relational comfort, seasons of like or dislike, or changing ways two people relate to each other. Marriage is a covenant relationship.

---

[7]   Christopher Yuan, *Holy Sexuality and the Gospel: Sex, Desire, and Relationships Shaped by God's Grand Story* (Colorado Springs: Multnomah, 2018), 87.

Ryan Andrew Smith

Between One Man and One Woman …

The marriage covenant is holy, meaning it is set apart by God for a distinct purpose. In Genesis 2, it isn't the man who creates and institutes marriage but God who ordains it for His glory and purposes. This means that marriage does not belong to people—it belongs to God. People may try to redefine marriage or use the word in a different way, but it is impossible to take from God's hands what is fully and rightfully His. God owns the true definition of marriage. People do not define or redefine what God has made, given, and purposed.

Foundational to this God-ordained marriage relationship is the fact that the marriage covenant is to be between one man and one woman. Just as God separated man from woman as two parts of the same image by creating gender, God purposes the reunion of the two image-bearers in marriage. The use of the word "reunion" is important. God does not just join two random people in marriage. He does not merely bless the commitment initiated by two individuals based on their attraction to each other, no matter how sincerely they run toward that goal. As Claus Westermann notes, "It should be stressed that the drive of the sexes toward each other is not the only element in the institution of marriage as we meet it in the Old Testament … Often it is not even the decisive element."[8]

When God reunifies a man and woman in marriage, it is not simply based on their drive or desire but on God's desire for unification of the separated *Imago Dei*—the image of God. This does not mean that single people do not carry and display the image of God. They certainly have the *Imago Dei* and display it in amazing ways! It simply means that God created marriage to display the connected *Imago Dei* between a man and a woman together.

---

[8]   Claus Westermann, *Genesis 1–11* (Minneapolis: Fortress Press, 1994), 233.

The author of Genesis notes that there was no animal that would satisfy what God desired for the man. After all, animals were not made in the image of God. What God wanted for the man had to be of identical worth and value in carrying the *Imago Dei*. Remember, in the image of God, He made *them*—male and female. As Adam declared, Eve was bone of *his* bones and flesh of *his* flesh. She was identical to him. Marriage is the union of two equal creatures.

Marriage is not just the union of any two equal creatures. God did not make a clone of Adam for His purpose to be fulfilled. Adam doesn't just need another Adam. Adam needs a helper that matches him. Eve was a helper—a complement. This word "helper" does not mean "lesser" or "inferior to." It's not a Robin to a Batman. The word "helper" is actually used of God Himself in the Old Testament in relation to His people. The word is more descriptive of someone who comes alongside someone else for a certain purpose.

To accomplish what God created Adam and Eve as humans to do, namely reproduce and raise more little image-bearers, Eve possessed every physical necessity that Adam did not have. Likewise, Adam had physical characteristics as a part of his gender that Eve did not have. The two could not accomplish God's design, order, and function alone. They had to have something outside of themselves to multiply and fill the earth. They needed very specific help to enable them to reproduce, and the opposite gender was created exactly with those specific things. God created male and female genders uniquely, and the reunification of the two is designed to accomplish His unique purpose, function, and design.

We could say that what God combines in the marriage covenant are *identical complementary opposites*. What does that mean? Those are big words for an actually very simple concept.

Let's go back to the puzzle pieces. How do you know that two puzzle pieces are meant to go together? First, you would have a general idea because they came from the same box. They are *identical* in substance. They are of the same "kind." They are puzzle pieces. They are made from the same material in the same factory. Since they came from the same box and are pieces of the same puzzle, you know they have the same general design, function, and purpose.

You wouldn't look for any puzzle piece in any box or any object that may be the same size to fit into a certain puzzle piece. You would need something that had an identical purpose. You would know two puzzle pieces were meant to go together, first, only if they were *identical.*

Second, just because you have two pieces doesn't mean they go together. You know two pieces go together if they unite to tell the same story or reflect the same image on the box. Both pieces need each other to display a greater part of the picture. They go with each other. They are *complementary.* If the pieces, when matched, don't create a continuous picture, you know something is off. You can look at the greater design—the picture on the box—and identify whether two pieces go together. First, you know by fit, but you also know by the part of the picture the two create. Puzzle pieces don't exist just for themselves but to image something greater.

There is something more at stake than just getting two pieces to smash together. They must not only fit, but they must fit in a way that unifies them for a greater purpose. You know two pieces go together if they are identical yet *complementary.*

Third, you wouldn't just put any two puzzle pieces together simply because they were made of cardboard, came from the same box, and look like they may be part of the same picture. Puzzle pieces have a design. Certain pieces are meant to go with other pieces. You know this because of their form. If you have a puzzle piece that has an open space, you don't look for a piece with another open space to align with it. You immediately look for a puzzle piece that is formed specifically to go into that open shape. The two types of pieces are different. They are created to go together *because* they are different—they are *opposites*. The two pieces only fit together because they are different. If they were too similar, they wouldn't fit. Because they are different or complementary yet identical, same in form, function, and purpose, you know the pieces are meant for each other.

Just because a puzzle piece has an opening doesn't mean that anything that fits that opening serves to fit the piece or the puzzle. If two pieces are not made of the same kind—matching in physical design, form, and function—or are not designated by a boundary marker, in this case a box, then you know they don't go together. They aren't identical.

Two pieces that are somewhat similar can be smashed together to pretty much fit. One may have an opening, and the other may fit an opening. They can be identical and opposite, but if they aren't complementary, the same part of the same image, then you know they ultimately don't belong with each other. They aren't complementary in design, form, and function.

If two pieces look similar in kind and appearance but don't have the same form or fittedness, you know they may be very close in image, but in function, they obviously don't go together. They aren't opposites. What is needed for puzzle pieces to work together individually is what also makes them work as a part of the greater puzzle—they are *identical complementary opposites*.

Bible scholar Dennis Hollinger notes, "[Marriage is] a union between two who are alike as fellow-humans, and yet unalike as male and female."[9]

This unique kind of union is affirmed by Jesus in Matthew 19. In this account, people are trying to trap Jesus by asking Him difficult social questions. Jesus is questioned about divorce, specifically how a man should best go about divorcing his wife.

Jesus's response is not just that they shouldn't divorce, though they shouldn't. Jesus highlights the necessity of the union

---

[9]   Yuan, *Holy Sexuality*, 85.

of identical complementary opposites in marriage. In answer to the question about divorce Jesus, states, "Have you not read that He who created them from the beginning made them male and female, and said, 'Therefore a man shall leave his father and his mother and hold fast to his wife, and the two shall become one flesh'? So they are no longer two but one flesh" (Matthew 19:4–6a ESV).

What Jesus describes as the marriage covenant is not just the joining of any two people but the uniting of a male and female as one flesh. The one-flesh union means many things, but at its base level, the one-flesh union means the physical act of sex. We will talk more about this in the next chapter, but for now, know that the act of sex is the physical sign that seals the marriage covenant. Yuan talks about this beautiful sexual union of a husband and wife as identical complementary opposites as he states, "The Bible upholds sexual purity as a tension between similarity and complementarity—similar but not too similar, different but not too different. This comes out clearly in certain prohibitions in Leviticus 18: incest is too *similar*, thus sinful; same-sex relationships are too *similar*, thus sinful; bestiality [sex with animals] is too *different*, thus sinful."[10]

Puzzle pieces need to fit in sameness and difference to accomplish their purpose as puzzle pieces. In the same way, to accomplish God's purposes in marriage, the two people being married need to fit in sameness and difference. Only men and women fit together in sameness and difference. Marriage is between male and female.

In All of Life for the Rest of Life

We will talk about this more in the next chapter, but what God does in giving sex as the defining physical marker of a marriage is

---

[10]   Ibid.

very important. Sex is the most intimate and vulnerable activity someone can participate in with another person. As such, sex is the perfect sign of the marriage covenant because it shows your spouse that you hold nothing back from them. You're literally naked before them physically and figuratively. Your marriage applies to all your life, not just certain segments of it. God is not divided in Himself. He exists in beautiful harmonious relationship in the Trinity. Similarly, men and women are to image God in marriage by not being divided in parts of their life. They are to exist in unhindered harmonious relationship. Marriage is for all of life.

Marriage is also to be permanent. It is common for a husband and wife to profess "'til death do us part" as a final proclamation in their wedding vows. God gives marriage to be a union for the rest of a couple's natural lives because they have responsibilities to each other and others for the rest of their natural lives.

God gives sex not just as a means of personal satisfaction or just to feel good but as a means of creating a new family reality. A family reality exists for someone's entire life. Parents never stop being parents even when their kids are grown. Kids never stop being kids even when they become adults. Husbands and wives aren't just husbands and wives as long as they're young and good-looking but also when they're old, wrinkled, and can barely see each other. Marriage is in all of life for the rest of life.

"Therefore a man shall leave his father and his mother and hold fast to his wife" (Genesis 2:24 ESV). By saying that a man should leave his family and hold fast to his wife in a new family, Genesis 2 shows that the making of this new family is to be in all of life for the rest of life. Grudem observes, "In [marriage] the man and woman promise each other that they will be faithful to this marriage for a lifetime, and they call God to witness their promise and to hold them accountable for being faithful to it."[11]

---

[11]   Grudem, *Christian Ethics*, 701.

Whereas, before his marriage commitment, a man's primary allegiance and obligation is to his parents; after his marriage commitment, his primary allegiance and obligation are to his wife.

MARRIAGE

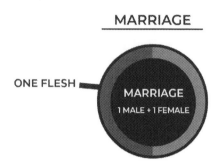

God's design for the family is vitally important to the purpose and function of humanity. That is why the family is so often attacked and distorted by Satan. If Satan can reorient our understanding of the family, marriage, and sex, then he can undermine the very foundations upon which we as humans are distinctly built. God's purpose and design in monogamous (only one man and one woman) heterosexual marriage serves to fulfill the purpose for which He created people. Even more than that, marriage is meant to be a beautiful picture of the gospel itself (we'll talk more about that later). Simply stated, God has given humanity an amazing, powerful, beautiful, and intentional gift in marriage.

It is important to note the fact that God's creation of two genders and the giving of the marriage covenant took place *before* sin entered the world in Genesis 3. After sin entered the world, like everything else in God's good creation, gender, sex, and marriage were broken by sin. However, they are not the products of sin. Instead, they call out to us today as echoes from Eden, reverberating music from the perfect creation God made, blessed, and said was very good.

Gender and marriage provide a glimpse into a pre-fall world in which God's sovereignly designed creation flourishes under His loving design.

Haven't Things Changed?

But haven't things changed? After all, we live in a different world than Adam and Eve did in Eden. We now have different desires. Our feelings change. If God's design for sex, gender, and marriage are Old Testament ideas, what about the New Testament? Surely God's circle of joy and protection for sex, gender, and sexuality should be bent or loosened to align better with the time and culture we find ourselves in today. Right?

God's design for sexuality and marriage is not just an Old Testament idea. If Jesus had wanted to loosen the boundaries of God's definition of sex, gender, and marriage, He had every opportunity to do so. If Jesus believed the Old Testament teaching on covenant was restrictive, out of date, and ready for a modern rebranding, He certainly could have done it. But He didn't.

In fact, Jesus did the opposite. Instead of loosening the definition of marriage and gender, Jesus actually closed the loopholes people were using to distort God's gift of marriage. Jesus upheld God's design and purpose for sex and sexuality above anyone's sexual "rights" or wants. Jesus wanted people to know that their sexual purity was more important than their sexual pleasure.

For example, in Matthew 5:27–28, Jesus says, "You have heard that it was said, 'You shall not commit adultery.' But I say to you that everyone who looks at a woman with lustful intent has already committed adultery with her in his heart" (ESV).

Rather than accommodate people's sin, Jesus tightened up the definition of sin. Likewise, Jesus talks about divorce in Mark

10:5–9, not by affirming the people's desires to break the marriage covenant, but by showing that the marital covenant is not to be broken. Jesus again roots this idea in the Genesis account as He explains that it was "because of your hardness of heart he wrote you this commandment. But from the beginning of creation, God made them male and female. 'Therefore a man shall leave his father and mother and hold fast to his wife, and the two shall become one flesh.' So they are no longer two but one flesh. What therefore God has joined together, let not man separate" (ESV).

At this idea of covenant faithfulness, the religious leaders questioning Jesus became extremely upset. They had bent God's truth to fit around their own passions and feelings. They had brought marriage down to their level where they could use it as they wanted, not as God had given it. In response, they scream at Jesus, "Well, if that's the case, it's better not to marry at all!"

Rather than bend to their ideas or satisfy their desires, Jesus basically responds, "OK. Yes, it may be unpopular or difficult to embrace, but it's true," as Jesus simply states "The one who is able to accept it should accept it" (Matthew 19:12 CSB).

Every time Jesus was questioned on an issue related to sex or marriage, He pointed back to Genesis 1 and 2. For Jesus, the circle of God's design, protection, and flourishing still held true even in a broken and sinful world. Jesus didn't treat the creation accounts as metaphorical stories, fiction, or bound to a certain cultural time and place. Jesus treated God's original design for the male and female sexes in Genesis 1 and God's union of the two in marriage as models for all human sexual behavior in all times, places, and cultures.

Interestingly, Jesus pointed not only to the marriage covenant in Genesis 2 as a basic argument against divorce, but He also linked the Genesis 1 creation of male and female genders as being central components of the marriage covenant. Jesus said "for this reason" in Mark 10:7 to connect His teaching with Genesis 2:24. *For this reason*—because God made them male and female as identical complementary opposites—man and woman may be joined in a permanent one-flesh union.

For Jesus, marriage was to be a sacred lifelong covenant between one man and one woman in all of life for the rest of life, just as it was defined in the beginning. Jesus confirmed that even in a different time, place, and culture, the circle still holds.

Not only does this common thread run through the Old Testament and into the gospels, but also the New Testament writers continue the theme of God's design for sex and sexuality. Paul tells Timothy in 1 Timothy 3:2 and 12 that to be a pastor or a deacon, a man must be faithful to his marriage with his one wife. In Ephesians 5, Paul puts a huge glaring spotlight on the marriage relationship, saying that, ultimately, the marriage covenant is not just an expression of love between two people, but it is, in fact, a picture of the gospel itself.

When Jesus, Paul, and the other New Testament writers appeal to the Old Testament to uphold marriage, they don't point to the polygamous (having many wives) kings of Israel as models. They don't point to King David, a man "after God's own heart," or to Solomon, the wisest king who ever lived (they both royally messed up sexually). They don't even point back to the polygamist patriarchs of Israel: Abraham, Isaac, and Jacob. As important as these figures and their marriages are to the Bible, neither Jesus, Paul, nor the other New Testament writers look to any of them as models for understanding marriage and sex. Instead, without exception, they look back to the pre-fall monogamous heterosexual uniting of Adam and Eve in Genesis 1–2 as the definition for flourishing human sexuality and marriage.[12]

Marriage is not a social construct or contract. Sex is not merely a means of physical pleasure. The apostle Paul says the marriage relationship is ultimately given by God as a picture of Christ's relationship with His church—His bride.

---

[12]   Denny Burk, *What Is the Meaning of Sex?* (Wheaton: Crossway, 2013), 88.

One way men and women can image God is through marriage. This means our simple human marriages on earth have cosmic supernatural implications in eternity. As Grudem explains, "If a husband commits adultery, He is portraying Christ as being unfaithful to His people, abandoning them, and not keeping His covenant with them. If a wife commits adultery, it is a picture of the church worshipping another god and being unfaithful to Christ. Both portrayals are deeply dishonoring to Christ."[13]

If this is true, what might it say if a society attempts to redefine what God has clearly defined as marriage? What about affirming the "marriage" of one man with another man or a woman with another woman? What about a man and three women? What about the man who keeps dumping his wives and moving on to new ones? What about the wife who is unloving toward her husband and seeks the attention of other men?

What may seem to some to be just a consenting relational declaration of love between two people is magnified to cosmic proportions in the Bible. The Scriptures are clear: sex, sexuality, and marriage are not insignificant. Holiness and purity in these areas are about much more than individual bents or desires. Marriage is ultimately an image of Christ and His people.

At this point, depending on your background, you may be sensing a degree of guilt or regret at how you have treated sex or marriage in the past. Had you known what you know now, you might have treated sex or marriage differently. Please know, my aim is not to make you feel guilty. Remember, Jesus had much, much grace with sexually broken people—the woman at the well, the prostitute who cried on His feet—who left their old passions behind to trust and follow Jesus in joyful and satisfying obedience. No matter where you've been, God calls you forward to trust and follow Jesus regarding your sex, gender, marriage, and sexuality. Start today.

---

[13]   Grudem, *Christian Ethics*, 713.

Grace and mercy are available through the cross of Jesus Christ. Jesus continually comforted broken and repentant people. As author Rebecca McLaughlin says, "While Jesus's condemnation of sexual sin is terrifying, his consistent welcome of repentant sexual sinners is equally shocking."[14]

But Jesus also never bent on the standard. Jesus always pointed back to the circle of God's definition regarding sex, gender, and sexuality. Not only did He not open it up to subjective expression, but Jesus also doubled down on God's objective definition. Again and again, the Bible defines God's circle of joy and protection in this way: Sex is the physical sign of a relational marriage covenant, and marriage is the covenant relationship between one man and one woman in all of life for the rest of life.

Jesus upheld the circle of God's definition and protection. Why? Because the sex you do or do not have, your gender, your marriage, and your sexuality are about much more than you. Your sex, gender, marriage, and sexuality, no matter what they are, are tools God has given you to share the gospel story of Christ and His church.

The ultimate goal of your gender, sexuality, marriage, and sex is to glorify God by imaging Christ. As the apostle Paul says in Ephesians 5:31–32, "'Therefore a man shall leave his father and mother and hold fast to his wife, and the two shall become one flesh.' This mystery is profound, and I am saying that it refers to Christ and the church" (ESV). Now that's a high call!

Your marriage, your gender, and your sexuality are not about you. They're about Jesus. For some people, the story of the gospel will be displayed in covenant biblical marriage. For others, it will be displayed in trusting and following Christ by using their singleness as a tool for the gospel just as Paul championed in 1 Corinthians 7. Both of those paths must be celebrated.

---

[14] Rebecca McLaughlin. *Confronting Christianity*. (Wheaton, ILL: Crossway, 2019), 166.

Ryan Andrew Smith

God's definition of and purpose for sex, gender, and marriage are not up to us to redefine. They are not personal or changeable. They are fixed and given by a good God for His glory and our joy. God designed marriage as the covenant relationship between one man and one woman in all of life for the rest of life, and it was good.

Questions for Further Study and Reflection

1. What is something you learned from this chapter?
2. Is the statement *"God designed marriage as the covenant relationship between one man and one woman in all of life for the rest of life"* controversial to you?
3. Why would our culture find the above statement controversial?
4. How have you seen people try to redefine God's design for marriage? What do you think God thinks about that?
5. How are you going to apply what you learned in this chapter?

PART 5

WHAT IS BIBLICAL SEX?

The Two Become One Flesh

Genesis 2:24 says the result of the marriage covenant is that the two become "one flesh." What does that mean? Whatever it means, it's important. Christopher Yuan explores this as he says, "This 'one flesh' concept is, by far, the most profound and fundamental statement on marriage in Scripture."[15]

At its core, the one-flesh union means God has given a physical sign to accompany the marriage relationship. This is consistent with the way God does things. God's covenants are always accompanied by a physical sign. God sealed the covenant with His people of Israel in the Old Testament by giving them the physical sign of circumcision. God also gave the physical sign of water baptism under the new covenant between Christ and His church.

God, as a covenant-making King, distinguishes covenants with a physical covenant sign. The act of sex between husband and wife is the physical act that represents their covenant union under God. Sex is the one-flesh union between a husband and wife.

---

[15]   Yuan, *Holy Sexuality*, 88.

While the one-flesh union may be more than just sex, it certainly isn't less. Consider Paul's warning to the church at Corinth: "Or do you not know that the one who joins himself to a prostitute is one body with her? For He says, 'the two shall become one flesh'" (1 Corinthians 6:16 NASB).

In this verse, Paul links the sexual act between a man and a prostitute with the one-flesh union in Genesis 2:24. What Paul is saying is that the one-flesh union is carried out through the physical act of sex. William Loader says, "Sexual intercourse actually changes people by creating a new reality; oneness with another person."[16]

Though sexual intercourse alone does not make a marriage, Wayne Grudem explains, "These passages remind us that God has never considered sexual intercourse to be an inconsequential, casual event. It involves not only a physical union but also a deep emotional and spiritual bonding that is only appropriate within the secure bounds of a lifelong, committed, faithful marriage relationship."[17]

Sex was created to exist only within the circle of a covenant marriage. Grudem also observes, "In the creation narrative, sex is always seen within the context of marriage, implying that it has belonged within marriage from the very beginning. This is clear from Genesis 2:24 … The phrase 'hold fast to *his wife*' implies that it is within the context of marriage that they 'become one flesh.'"[18] What this means is that because of their sexual union, two people engaging in sex are no longer two but are now "one flesh."

Let's go back to the Hebrew for a minute. The Hebrew word for "flesh" in Genesis 2:24 is *basar.* The word *basar* refers to the entirety of a person or relationship between two people, not just

---

[16]   William Loader, *The Septuagint, Sexuality, and the New Testament* (Grand Rapids: Eerdman's, 2004), 90-92.

[17]   Grudem, *Christian Ethics*, 703.

[18]   Ibid.

Ryan Andrew Smith

physical bodily flesh. Therefore, Adam and Eve's marriage was to be more than just physical sex. Instead, their union was to be an all-encompassing reality that fused two separate individuals into a new singular unit—a family.[19]

There are three main areas in which the one-flesh union is carried out between husband and wife. First, the one-flesh union is about companionship. A husband and wife should be friends. The book of Proverbs talks about the blessing of a godly spouse as it says, "He who finds a wife finds a good thing and obtains favor from the Lord" (Proverbs 18:22 ESV).

The Scripture says that married couples should be joyful in their youth and enjoy the benefits of companionship in marriage. Couples should spend time together, watch movies with each other, eat ice cream together, and talk to each other about life. As one flesh, a husband and wife share their one life together.

Second, the Bible calls married couples to enjoy the physical aspects of sex in their one-flesh union. This truth is woven into the very bodies of the male and female genders. God made sex feel good. The writer of Proverbs declares, "Let your fountain be blessed, and rejoice in the wife of your youth, a lovely deer, a graceful doe. Let her breasts fill you at all times with delight; be intoxicated always in her love" (Proverbs 5:18–19 ESV). Remember, God made sex as a part of His "very good" creation. Sex was meant to be *enjoyed* between husband and wife.

Last, the one-flesh union means a new family exists in which children may be born through the act of sex. The fact that human reproduction happens through sex, and sex is to go along with a marriage covenant, means that God wants children to be born into and raised within a family already established by the one-flesh marriage covenant. In other words, kids should be born into families.

Even though the one-flesh union is much more than sex, that doesn't mean that the importance of sex within the one-flesh

[19]   Yuan, *Holy Sexuality,* 89.

marriage is lessened. Sex is a physical act that as a sign is much greater than just a physical act. When two people physically become one, it is a celebration of their complete union together. They share each other as they share their whole lives. This makes sex truly meaningful.

The idea that sex is insignificant or can be just casual is completely opposite to the Bible's teaching on sex and sexuality. Considering Jesus's words, it is also contradictory to think that sex between two men or two women can accomplish the same type of one-flesh union that God gave at the beginning of creation. Yuan says,

> If all Jesus wanted to reaffirm was the indivisibility of marriage, the "one flesh" imagery from Genesis 2:24 would've been sufficient. But Jesus introduces the biblical concept of sexual differentiation from Genesis 1:27, which on the surface doesn't seem directly relevant: "God made them male and female" (Mark 10:6). Yet for Jesus, it's immensely relevant: There's no marriage apart from the biblical paradigm of male and female. Jesus tethers the creation of "male and female" (Genesis 1:27) to the creation of "one flesh" marriage (Genesis 2:24). This beautifully illustrates that God both differentiates male and female at creation and unites male and female in marriage. Jesus is affirming that when God made male and female, our Creator already had in mind the marital union that followed.[20]

---

[20]   Yuan, *Holy Sexuality,* 91.

The importance of sex is seen throughout the rest of the Bible. In Exodus 20:14, God gives the eighth commandment: "You shall not commit adultery" (ESV). "Adultery" in English is translated from the Hebrew word *na'aph* (You had no idea you were going to become such a Hebrew scholar by reading this book, did you?), which means engaging sexually with any woman who is the wife or fiancé of another man.[21]

Again, what we see is that God has created sex to be enjoyed only within the context of marriage. Jesus affirmed the terrible nature of adultery by listing it in Matthew 15:19 alongside murder, theft, and lying as evidence of a broken and evil heart. Jesus also reemphasized the command against adultery in Matthew 19:8 and Luke 18:20.

In Romans 2:22, the apostle Paul compares adultery to the worship of false idols (idolatry) which is done in the face of and as an affront to God Himself. James, the half-brother of Jesus, spoke out against sex outside of marriage as well (see James 2:11). The writer of Proverbs raises a flashing bright red warning light when it comes to sex outside of marriage as he tells the reader to run from dishonoring the marriage vow or using sex in any way outside of the marriage covenant. Proverbs 6:32–33 warns, "He who commits adultery lacks sense; he who does it destroys himself. He will get wounds of dishonor, and his disgrace will not be wiped away" (ESV).

Cheating on a spouse is just like cheating on God. Even though people may feel strong urges to have sex outside of the marriage covenant, those urges should be denied. There is too much at stake. As author Rebecca McLaughlin explains, "Most Christians struggle at times with attractions that, if followed, would lead them into sexual sin. In this respect, we're all in the same boat. But if the faithful one-flesh union of a man and

---

[21]   William L. Holladay, Walter Baumgartner, and Ludwig Köhler. *A Concise Hebrew and Aramaic Lexicon of the Old Testament.* (Grand Rapids: Eerdman's, 1989), 224.

a woman pictures Christ's marriage to His church, any sexual relationship outside that model pictures idolatry. Without boundary lines, there is no image."[22]

God demands that sex within the marriage covenant be kept holy. This means sex should be had only according to its original purpose. Adultery tries to bring another person into the one-flesh union that God created to be between one man and one woman. Sex outside of marriage abuses the physical sign of the covenant by calling God to observe a covenantal pledge that neither person has any intention of keeping. Sex outside of marriage mocks God, scoffs at His creation, and abuses His good gift. Sex outside of the marriage context is empty. It's hollow.

Sex is the distinguishing physical sign of a marriage, a covenant union, between husband and wife. It is the physical reunification of the two pieces that God separated then united. The purpose of sex is to physically represent the spiritual, covenantal reality of marriage. Married people should have sex. Sex should be had between married people. God made sex and clearly defined it in the very beginning. "And God saw everything that He had made," including our bodies, minds, sex, and marriage, "and behold, it was very good" (Genesis 1:31 ESV).

---

[22] McLaughlin. *The Secular Creed,* 35.

Questions for Further Study and Reflection

1. What is something you learned from this chapter?
2. How would our culture define *sex*?
3. What would happen in our world if everyone lived according to the Bible's definition of sex?
4. Why would adultery be like idolatry?
5. How are you going to apply what you learned in this chapter?

PART 6

WHAT ISN'T BIBLICAL SEXUALITY?

Recognizing the Counterfeits

If biblical sexuality is so important and relevant today, why doesn't the Bible address today's biggest concerns like transgenderism or a gender spectrum? The Bible doesn't talk about online porn or virtual reality sex in the metaverse. Can such an old document possibly understand and speak to the realities of today?

Here's the truth: The Bible is more concerned with conveying the *reality* of sex, gender, and sexuality (the circle) than the *counterfeits*—or every possibility that could exist outside the circle.

Here's a helpful illustration: When law enforcement officers are trained to identify forged dollar bills, they don't go into a room with every possible way a person could forge a dollar. After all, someone could always come up with a new and more clever way to copy a Benjamin. Instead, in training to identify counterfeits, law enforcement officers spend time with real dollar bills. They learn the real thing so they can identify the counterfeits. They hold real bills in their hands. They learn to identify the touch, feel, and smell of real currency. Their eyes become used to the intricate design, print, and materials. They can easily identify counterfeits because they have spent their time with the real thing.

In the same way, the Bible identifies *some* of the counterfeits of God's design for sex, gender, and sexuality, but those it does not directly address are not any less counterfeits. The truth is that the Bible is more concerned with focusing on the circle itself rather than chasing every possible thing outside of it.

Porneia: Distortions of God's Design

The Bible has a single word in Greek that describes *anything* and *everything* outside the circle of God's design and protection. All kinds of sexual deviance, all the counterfeits, are referred to in the Bible under one umbrella using the Greek word *porneia* (note the similarity to our word *pornography*). *Porneia* is usually translated in our English Bibles as "sexual immorality." *Porneia* is the general term used by the Bible's writers to refer to anything outside of the circle.

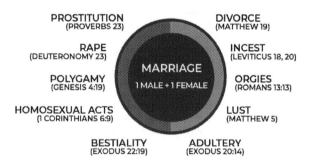

'PORNEIA'
ANYTHING OUTSIDE GOD'S DESIGN

PROSTITUTION
(PROVERBS 23)

DIVORCE
(MATTHEW 19)

RAPE
(DEUTERONOMY 23)

INCEST
(LEVITICUS 18, 20)

MARRIAGE
1 MALE + 1 FEMALE

POLYGAMY
(GENESIS 4:19)

ORGIES
(ROMANS 13:13)

HOMOSEXUAL ACTS
(1 CORINTHIANS 6:9)

LUST
(MATTHEW 5)

BESTIALITY
(EXODUS 22:19)

ADULTERY
(EXODUS 20:14)

The word *porneia* is used twenty-six times in the New Testament. Other forms of the word are used about thirty times throughout the text. Let me give you just a few examples.

In Matthew 5:32 and 19:9, Jesus uses the word to talk about the only time divorce is allowable. The apostles encourage gentiles to run away from *porneia* several times in the book of Acts. Paul condemns the church at Corinth for the *porneia* they are allowing to exist even among their own church (a man was sleeping with his mom ... I know ...).

Paul continues to urge the people at Corinth to remember that the body is not meant for *porneia* (1 Corinthians 6:13). Paul addresses the temptation toward *porneia* and mourns over those who are chasing it to find joy and fulfillment (2 Corinthians 12:21). To the church at Colossae, Paul boldly writes that they should put *porneia* to death. He urges, "Therefore, put to death what belongs to your earthly nature: sexual immorality [*porneia*], impurity, lust, evil desire, and greed, which is idolatry" (Colossians 3:5 CSB).

As you can see, the Bible gives bright red flashing warning signs and uses its harshest words to warn against *porneia*. The Bible warns its readers against abusing sex and stepping outside of God's covenant circle of joy and protection. Perhaps nowhere is this more clearly seen than in Paul's letter to the church at Corinth:

> Flee from sexual immorality [*porneia*]. Every other sin a person commits is outside the body, but the sexually immoral person sins against his own body. Or do you not know that your body is a temple of the Holy Spirit within you, whom you have from God? You are not your own, for you were bought with a price. So glorify God in your body (1 Corinthians 6:18–20 ESV).

The Bible records several times in which God's people throw aside or distort God's design for marriage, sex, and gender. Just two chapters after God creates marriage in Genesis 2, a man named Lamech takes two wives instead of one, attempting to redefine marriage using his own wants and desires (Genesis 4:19). While the Old Testament accounts that follow are littered with polygamy (having multiple husbands or wives) even among those who are supposed to be following God, the biblical examples of polygamy bristle with jealousy, fighting, rivalry, heartache, and even murder. Stepping outside of God's circle never ends well.

Further counterfeits show the downward spiral of sexual sin and the breaking of the marriage covenant. Exodus 22:10 addresses bestiality. Leviticus 19:29 warns against sexual promiscuity (having "casual" sex outside of marriage). Deuteronomy 22:5 protects male/female identities and says not to cross-dress. Likewise, Deuteronomy 22:13–21, 28–29, and Exodus 22:16–17 all speak to the importance of protecting one's virginity before marriage.

While the Bible does not address every possible thing that could lie outside the circle of God's design and protection, its message is clear: What God has designed, humanity has broken in multiple ways. However, because of His love, God still calls His people to His unbreakable standard for His glory and our good.

Does God Punish Sexual Sin?

No one likes punishment. Punishment seems mean. Would God really punish us for doing something He tells us not to do? Isn't that what Zeus and the ancient gods did? Is the one true God really going to punish us for sin?

The truth is, in any kind of world where right and wrong exist, punishment must exist as a way to direct people toward what is right and keep them away from what is wrong. A parent might punish their child for running into the street. This is done to keep the child from future danger and to protect them within the bounds of what is safe. Our stomachs might punish us for over-indulging in some late-night Arby's. This is a natural result, a punishment, from our bodily system telling us that what we have put in our body is not what it needs.

What if there was a completely perfect, right, honest, and loving judge who cared for his people and wanted them to enjoy the path of what is good and true? Wouldn't he punish people for doing wrong? What if there was a loving and concerned father who always did what was best for his children? Wouldn't he lovingly encourage his kids when they did what was right and lovingly correct them when they were heading the wrong way? In this way, the father's punishment would not really be punishment as much as it would be loving guidance.

The good news is that the Bible says God is that type of good and righteous judge who provides consequences so that we will see what is right and true and what is wrong and false. He is our good Father who wants us to trust Him and see the benefits of living according to His ways. He does this because He loves us and wants us to enjoy life in His kingdom rather than suffer the hardships of trying to build our own kingdoms, which can never truly stand.

God is the righteous judge. He is the loving Father. He is the King who welcomes us into His home as His children. With God, there is life. Apart from God, there is no hope.

Rebellion against God

The reason *porneia* is destructive for the person who engages in it is that ultimately sexual sin is rebellion against a holy God who loves and is passionate about His people and His glory. "Do you not know?" Paul asks six times in 1 Corinthian 6 as he urges Christians to run from sexual immorality. Paul says in his letter to the Romans that people do recognize God's right and perfect ways but would rather exchange them for their own ways. He relates,

> For they exchanged the truth of God for a lie, and worshiped and served the creature rather than the Creator, who is blessed forever. Amen. For this reason God gave them over to degrading passions; for their women exchanged the natural function for that which is unnatural, and in the same way also the men abandoned the natural function of the woman and burned in their desire toward one another, men with men committing indecent acts and receiving in their own persons the due penalty of their error ... and although they knew the ordinance of God, that those who practice such things are worthy of death, they not only do the same, but also give hearty approval to those who practice them (Romans 1:25–27, 32 NASB).

What Paul is saying at the end of Romans 1 is that people *do* know God's righteous decrees, the ways of creation, yet still willfully try to act against them. We try to fight against God.

When followers of Christ speak out against various kinds of *porneia,* they are not just speaking out *against* a person's feelings or autonomy. Instead, they are speaking out *for* that person's eternal, spiritual, physical, and emotional state. True Christians don't want others to be cut off from eternal life on either side of heaven.

When Jesus absorbed the just and righteous wrath of God on behalf of those He came to save, He absorbed it all. His death was sufficient to cover the punishment for our sin. Jesus invites His rebellious enemies to be His children. However, not all rebels will surrender to the true King and will suffer the consequences of that decision. The Bible is clear that there will be many people who experience the eternal wrath of God for willful and open rebellion against their Creator. Jesus explains this in the closing chapters of Revelation:

> To the thirsty I will give from the spring of water of life without payment. The one who conquers will have this heritage, and I will be his God and he will be my son. But as for the cowardly, the faithless, the detestable, as for murderers, *the sexually immoral*, sorcerers, idolaters, and all liars, their portion will be in the lake that burns with fire and sulfur, which is the second death (Revelation 21:6–8 ESV, emphasis added).

Christians do not want others to face God's wrath. That's why they echo Christ's call to "repent for the kingdom of heaven is at hand" (Matthew 3:2; 4:17 ESV).

Paul and the other New Testament writers don't warn people to flee from sexual immorality because they are killjoys or prudes. Acts of sexual deviation are, in fact, acts of rebellion against God. Gordon Fee notes:

> Sexual immorality is still sin, even though it has been justified under every conceivable rationalization. Those who take Scripture seriously are not prudes or legalists at this point. Instead, they recognize that God has purchased His people for higher things. Our bodies belong to God through the redemption of the

> cross, and they are destined for resurrection. One reason Christians flee sexual immorality is that their bodies are *for* the Lord, who is to be honored in the deeds of the body as well as in all other behavior and attitudes. [23]

As Romans 1 shows, when someone chooses to have a low and distorted view of God, they naturally develop an over-inflated and distorted view of themselves.

When we take our eyes off God, we always turn them to ourselves. We try to write our own story instead of seeing that we are already a part of a much greater and bigger story. Instead of seeking truth and what is right, we say our feelings are truth and that we can determine what is right for ourselves, even if that is different from what someone else says is true and right.

But there can only be one truth. Whatever is true is true. To walk away from that is to walk on a path into a dangerous world. It would be like the kid who believes he can fly. While that belief may seem cute, fun, and inspiring for a while, at some point, it becomes dangerous. Eventually, he'll find a roof.

In the same way, setting our lives on a trajectory guided only by our passions and feelings will ultimately get us lost in a world of self-deception. Sadly, because we can become so hardheaded and determined to follow our own path, at some point, God will let us do it and suffer the natural consequences in the end. This is not only the punishment we deserve, but it's also the punishment we ask for. Though we may fall into the pit of our own digging, fortunately for us, God doesn't leave us there.

Sadly, as Paul points out in Romans 1:32, a person's self-deception does not just impact that person alone. Self-deception spreads and demands to be validated. Those who exchange God's

---

[23] Gordon D. Fee, *The First Epistle to the Corinthians,* Rev. ed. The New International Commentary on the New Testament (Grand Rapids: Eerdmans, 2014), 294.

truth for their passions usually encourage others to affirm their choices or to join them in their pursuit. Culture for all is often driven by the demands of a few.

We were not made to be God. We cannot carry the weight of being God. When we try, we are eventually crushed under that weight. Whenever someone decides what is right or wrong based on what looks good to them or seems better than God's true path of righteousness, they are not forging a new path of freedom. They are simply following the old well-worn road of Adam and Eve that leads to physical and spiritual death.

Satan's tactic against God's good design and circle of protection in the garden of Eden was to make God's way seem restrictive. "Did God actually say, 'you shall not eat of any tree in the garden?'" asked the serpent (Genesis 3:1 ESV).

Rather than pointing to God's good and generous design, the snake focused Eve's eyes on the restrictiveness of God's command. God said a thousand *yesses*. Satan focused on the one *no*.

Eden was a perfect world that protected Adam and Eve from destruction. In the fall, the perfect world became broken. Everything was affected. Rather than leave His creation in its sin, however, God continued to provide a circle of protection. God's circle kept life, truth, and protection on the inside, while death called to God's people from the outside.

Here's the truth: Whether what it says is popular or not, the Bible is clear on matters of sex, marriage, and sexuality. Deviation from God's design for sexuality is physically, emotionally, and spiritually destructive. Sex matters, and sex matters to God.

Our Sexual Line

Some may argue that God's designs for sex, gender, marriage, and sexuality are restrictive. They may believe that God's ways are legalistic, stifling, and require us to not be true to who we feel we really are. After all, isn't it wrong to draw lines of right and wrong for other people?

The truth is that everyone draws a line. Everyone abides by a circle of protection for sex and sexuality. Our culture's line is constantly moving, and many people simply move along with it. Whether you know it or not, depending on your worldview, you trust *a* circle for sex, marriage, and sexuality.

Let's do an experiment. What would you say to the married man who finds himself attracted to another woman? You likely would not encourage him to follow that lustful desire, even though he may feel defenseless against it. We understand deep down inside of us that adultery is across some kind of line. It isn't right, and it isn't good.

What would you say to the woman who wants to use her body for money or attention? You probably would not encourage her to become a prostitute. There is something innate within you that knows cheap sex for money is across some kind of line.

To the university student who has sexual thoughts about the girl in class, you probably wouldn't just say "boys will be boys" and encourage him down any sexual path he may desire. When it comes to sexuality, we know some things are right and some things are wrong. Some things are outside *our* circle.

The question is, how do you decide what is inside and what is outside your circle? What if someone told you that your circle was restrictive? How would you justify having any circle at all?

Wherever you would draw that line for yourself, you must be willing to ask from where you get that line. Our lines can be defined or influenced by others. We can also draw them for ourselves based on our own feelings and desires. Or we can let our line be determined by a good God who speaks to His broken creation through the Bible and has done so for thousands of years.

Either way, we are all trusting a circle. The question is whether it is the right circle, and the consequences are tremendous.

QUESTIONS FOR FURTHER STUDY AND REFLECTION

1. What is something you learned from this chapter?
2. What is a type of *porneia* that people agree is bad? Why do they feel that way about it? Are there some types of *porneia* people think are OK? What is the difference between the types of *porneia* that people think are bad and those they think are OK?
3. How have you developed your sexual line or circle of definition regarding sex and sexuality?
4. What would happen if your definition of what was right about sex and sexuality was not the same as God's definition? What would happen in your life if you changed it to align with God's definition?
5. How are you going to apply what you learned in this chapter?

PART 7

GOD'S CALL TO BIBLICAL SEXUALITY

Where Are We?

This may be the most important thing you read in this entire book. If I have explained everything up to this point adequately, yet neglected to communicate this truth, then I have completely failed you, myself, and most importantly, God.

Where are you and I when it comes to God's circle of joy and protection for sex and sexuality?

'PORNEIA'

PROSTITUTION
(PROVERBS 23)

DIVORCE
(MATTHEW 19)

RAPE
(DEUTERONOMY 23)

INCEST
(LEVITICUS 18, 20)

POLYGAMY
(GENESIS 4:19)

MARRIAGE
1 MALE + 1 FEMALE

ORGIES
(ROMANS 13:13)

HOMOSEXUAL ACTS
(1 CORINTHIANS 6:9)

LUST
(MATTHEW 5)

BESTIALITY
(EXODUS 22:19)

ADULTERY
(EXODUS 20:14)

The truth is, we are all outside the circle.

The book of Romans says, "*All* have sinned and fall short of the glory of God" (Romans 3:23 ESV, emphasis added).

In the Sermon on the Mount, Jesus said, "You have heard that it was said, 'Do not commit adultery.' But I say to you, everyone who looks at a woman with lustful intent has already committed adultery with her in his heart" (Matthew 5:27–28 ESV).

Jesus says that you may have never actually committed physical adultery, but even the lustful desire for sex outside of God's good design for marriage is adultery. This is true because what is broken is not just our acts but our hearts and very selves as well.

Because of our broken hearts and disordered affections, none of us are sexually perfect, holy, or righteous. We are *all* outside the circle at the foot of the cross. We may not be attracted to *all* types of *porneia,* but we may be drawn to some. Biblically speaking, one person's desire to look at heterosexual porn is no different from someone else's desire to have homosexual sex. It is all *porneia* according to the scripture. Our hearts, our affections, and our sexuality are broken—all of it, all of us.

While those feelings and attractions may be *what* we have, they are not *who* we are. As Sam Allberry states, "Desires for things God has forbidden are a reflection of how sin has distorted me, not how God has made me."[24]

Our brokenness is not what defines us. It is not what we must be or do. Regardless of how we are, what our thought life is, or what we are attracted to, we are called to sexual holiness; to live in light of *what* we are called to be, which are redeemed, renewed creations in Christ.

"What other options do we have," asks Christopher Yuan, a same-sex attracted Christian, choosing not to give in to his bent

---

[24]   Sam Allberry. *Is God Anti-Gay?* (Charlotte, NC: The Good Book Company), 30.

but to live within God's circle of protection for gender, sex, and marriage, "other than heterosexuality and homosexuality? What we need is a completely new paradigm to represent God's sexual ethic: *Holy Sexuality*."[25]

Sexual holiness is not defined as a married couple living in the suburbs with two kids and a dog. Sexual holiness is not making same-sex attracted people into opposite-sex attracted people, though that may happen. Remember, someone can commit a whole host of *porneia* even as a heterosexually married man or woman. The goal is not just faithfulness to an individual or simply being a kind person. Rebecca McLaughlin reminds us:

> There's no reason for a Christian to think that someone in a gay relationship is not also kind, generous, and trustworthy. A gay person might well be all these things, just as a straight person who commits adultery might be a nice person in other respects. We might have a gay friend who is faithful to his husband and a straight friend who is not faithful to his wife. If this surprises us, we might need to repent of our prejudice. *But we shouldn't repent of our theology*[26] (emphasis added).

The goal is not just heterosexuality but *holy* sexuality.

God's designs are perfect because God is perfect. God's purposes are holy because God is holy. Even though sin has entered God's creation and distorted God's design in the eyes of His people, God's standard and call still remain true: "Be holy, for I am holy" (Leviticus 11:45 ESV). But can we still really be holy in a broken world?

---

[25]   Yuan, *Holy Sexuality*, 47.

[26]   McLaughlin, *The Secular Creed*, 55.

Christopher Yuan helps us see what sexual holiness looks like for followers of Christ with broken bodies, broken minds, and distorted passions in a fallen world. He states, "From Genesis to Revelation, in the entirety of the Biblical witness, only two paths align with God's standard for sexual expression: if you're single, be sexually abstinent while fleeing lustful desires; if you're married, be sexually and emotionally faithful to your spouse of the opposite sex while also fleeing lustful desires."[27]

According to Yuan, holy sexuality consists of two paths: chastity in singleness and faithfulness in marriage. He explains, "Chastity is more than simply abstention from extramarital sex; it conveys purity and holiness. Faithfulness is more than merely maintaining chastity and avoiding illicit sex; it conveys covenantal commitment."[28]

The greatest covenant God calls His people to enter is not the marriage covenant, but an even greater covenant with God in Christ. The marriage covenant is merely a shadow, an echo, and an expression of this much greater covenant. Holy Sexuality expresses our allegiance to God's covenant more than any other covenant with a person.

Holy Sexuality for the Sexually Promiscuous, Same-Sex Attracted, or Gender-Dysphoric Person

What then does God call us as sexual sinners to do and become? God does not simply demand that our desires be magically changed. For some people, that may not happen. God does not simply call the same-sex attracted to be opposite-sex attracted. He does not just call the single person to marriage. What Jesus makes clear in the Sermon on the Mount is that the person with heterosexual lust in his heart is no different from the

---

[27]   Ibid., 48.
[28]   Ibid.

one steeped in adultery. We are all sexually broken sinners in need of redemption. The ground is very level at the foot of the cross.

God's call to holiness extends beyond just the heterosexual married couple. God called the Ethiopian eunuch to salvation in Acts 8. A eunuch was someone who had been forcefully or willingly castrated (had their testicles removed or crushed) to serve in a certain role. Eunuchs did not have a normal sexual drive because of their physical alteration or natural impairment. According to modern definitions, they would have been considered gender asexual or gender queer.

Jesus explains to His disciples, "There are eunuchs who have been so from birth, and there are eunuchs who have been made eunuchs by men, and there are eunuchs who have made themselves eunuchs for the sake of the kingdom of heaven. Let the one who is able to receive this receive it" (Matthew 19:12 ESV).

Whether they were castrated males or people physically incapable of having a sexual drive and function, eunuchs were still called by Jesus to live in holiness, including holy sexuality.

This same call is echoed by the apostle Paul in his letter to the Corinthians in which he talks a lot about sex and sexuality. After talking about sexuality and saving grace through Christ, Paul encourages unmarried widows to remain single.

What is clear from these passages is that there is ample room for the single adult to be welcomed under the banner of holy sexuality. There is room for the same-sex attracted and the opposite-sex attracted person in God's call to holiness and holy sexuality. "The truth is that God's standard for *everyone* is holy sexuality," Yuan explains. "The purpose of this phrase is to transcend the current secular paradigm of sexual orientation that is unable to point toward God's clear intent for sexual expression."[29]

At this point, a clear distinction must be made. Holy sexuality involves upholding God's original design for sex, gender, and the covenant marital relationship. What God instituted in Genesis

---

[29]   Yuan, *Holy Sexuality,* 48.

1 and 2, and defends throughout scripture, is that marriage is between one man and one woman in all of life for the rest of life. Sex is to be solely understood as the physical sign of that marriage covenant. To deny any of those central tenets is to be removed from God's circle of protection, to walk away from His goodness, embrace sexual sin, and ultimately, try to fight against God.

To divorce and break the covenant bond of marriage, except for certain circumstances,[30] is to fight against God. To use sex in any way other than as a sign of the marriage covenant is to fight against God. The sexual act between one man and another man or one woman with another woman is fighting against God. To marry one man with two women, a woman with a horse, a toaster with a penguin, or any other distortion of the one-man-one-woman covenant bond in all of life for the rest of life is an attempt to fight against God. The Bible is clear on this, and I hope I am as well.

Yet in a fallen world with broken desires, we may still experience a draw to live outside of God's design for sexuality and the marriage covenant. God's call to holy sexuality does not mean that homosexual desires will immediately disappear when someone comes to Christ. God calls us to relational holiness, to treat others the way we would want to be treated, when we surrender to Christ, but it doesn't mean we never have a bad feeling against someone. We still get angry. We still feel hurt. We have urges to step outside of God's relational design and injure or inflict payback on others. But when we surrender to Christ, God the Spirit begins to work within us to change us. It's a process. It doesn't happen overnight. But though our urges may remain in some areas, the way we respond to those urges does change.

---

[30] See Jesus's comments in Matthew 5:32, 19:9; Mark 10:11; and Luke 16:18. Trustworthy biblical scholars may disagree on the application of these words, specifically when pertaining to abuse and abandonment. That discussion is beyond the scope of this book. Certainly, however, we can agree that sexual immorality is a breach of the marriage covenant and can be interpreted as biblical grounds for divorce.

Sometimes the urges themselves are changed. Paul reminded the church at Corinth of this important truth:

> Or do you not know that the unrighteous will not inherit the kingdom of God? Do not be deceived: Neither the sexually immoral [*porneia*], nor idolaters, nor adulterers, nor men who practice homosexuality, nor thieves, nor the greedy, nor drunkards, nor revilers, nor swindlers will inherit the kingdom of God. *And such were some of you.* But you were washed, you were sanctified, you were justified in the name of the Lord Jesus Christ and by the Spirit of our God (1 Corinthians 6:9–11, ESV, emphasis added).

The apostle Paul told the church at Corinth in a later letter, "Therefore, if anyone is in Christ, he is a new creation. The old has passed away; behold the new has come" (2 Corinthians 5:17 ESV).

Paul likewise tells the Romans, "But thanks be to God, that you who were once slaves of sin have become obedient from the heart to the standard of teaching to which you were committed" (Romans 6:17 ESV).

If anyone is concerned that God can't or won't do such a work in them, Paul reminds the church at Philippi, "It is *God* who works in you, both to will and to work for *His* good pleasure" (Philippians 2:13 ESV, emphasis added).

John also reminds his readers, "If we confess our sins, He is faithful and just to forgive us our sins and to cleanse us from all unrighteousness" (1 John 1:9 ESV).

Holy sexuality is possible not because all desires are capable of reorientation, but because Christians are not slaves to their desires. In Christ and by the power of the Spirit, *all* people are able to walk in sexual holiness. Paul concludes, "Let not sin therefore reign in your mortal body, to make you obey its passions. Do not present your members to sin as instruments for unrighteousness, but present yourselves to God as those who have been brought from death to life, and your members to God as instruments for righteousness. For sin will have no dominion over you" (Romans 6:12–14 ESV).

God's call to live in holy sexuality is not just some lofty theological concept. The gospels put flesh on God's appeal to the sexually broken to walk in sexual holiness. Luke 7:36–50 (ESV) records the "woman of the city, who was a sinner" who turned away from her sexual brokenness and anointed Jesus's feet with ointment and tears. Jesus upheld her as an example of saving faith and repentance.

John 4 records Jesus speaking to a woman who had broken the marital covenant multiple times and was currently engaging in sex outside of any marital covenant at all. Not only does Jesus engage her in kind and charitable discussion, but He also calls her to leave behind dry wells and drink from the living water of holiness in Christ.

Luke 15:22–24 tells us about a father's unrestrained acceptance of a son who returned to him after engaging in all types of sexual sin. We may also think of Rahab the prostitute, whose faith in God is commended in Hebrews 11:31; the eunuch from Acts 8; as well as the tax collectors, sinners, and prostitutes Jesus and His disciples were rebuked for befriending. In all of these instances, what the Bible makes clear is that gospel hope is available for the sexually broken who would turn from their sin and embrace holy sexuality through Christ, by the power of the Spirit.

Jesus aggressively hated sin. Yet Jesus also aggressively loved and reached out toward those who would turn from their sin and come home to their good heavenly Father.

God's Grace for the Sexually Broken

The picture so far for anyone reading this book may seem bleak.

I get it. I'm a broken sinner. My attractions are disoriented, my past is littered with regret that I can't go back and change, and the only thing I have to look forward to is fighting more sin in my broken heart or facing judgment. Is there anything left for broken sinners like me?

Yes. I promise you, there is. For those asking that question, the Bible has a strong and certain word for you: *Hope.*

"But God ..." These words erupt from Paul's pen in Ephesians 2:4 after he has closed every conceivable door of hope for those who have followed the loud, vibrant course of this world that leads to death and disobedience. He states,

> And you were dead in the trespasses and sins in which you once walked, following the course of this world, following the prince of the power of the air, the spirit that is now at work in the sons of disobedience—among whom we all once lived in the passions of our flesh, carrying out the desires of the body and the mind and were by nature children of wrath, like the rest of mankind. *But God* ... (Ephesians 2:1–4 ESV, emphasis added).

These words echo in the readers' weary ears as Paul details the good news of the gospel of Jesus Christ who absorbed the wrath, took the penalty we deserved from a just judge, and died in our place on a cross.

Just as we died with Christ, Paul says Jesus also raised us with Him to walk in new resurrected life. This is the good news of the gospel. There is good news for all those who, like me, are sexually broken. God is a God of goodness and mercy. God extends His grace to the sexually broken.

God never leaves us in our sin. He calls us out of darkness and *into* light. God has a future for us. As we often say in our church, "It's OK not to be OK, but it's not OK to stay that way."

Because God the Holy Spirit is given to those who trust in Christ, all those who are saved are being made new (2 Corinthians 5:14–17). Likewise, those who belong to God through saving faith in Jesus Christ are set free from the former ways that bound them to eternal judgment and a bent toward sin (Colossians 3:5–11). Instead, they are invited to love and live within God's good, perfect, protective created design.

Sexual Restoration

God's call to the sexually broken person, which should also be the call extended from the church, is not "go and change" but "come and be transformed." As Paul says in Romans 12:2, "Do not be conformed to this world but be transformed by the renewal of your mind, that by testing you may discern what is the will of God, what is good and acceptable and perfect" (ESV).

The Bible is very honest with us: We are all broken and cannot fix ourselves. We need someone who is not broken to rescue us just as a drowning man in the ocean can't save himself or be saved by another drowning man. But only God is not broken. Only God can rescue us. The big question of the Bible is whether all that was broken in the fall can be restored. The big answer to that question is *yes*!

God the Son became a man. Jesus was 100 percent God and 100 percent man. He had to become a man because, justly, a human had to pay the price for humanity's sin. Jesus was tempted in every way we are but was without sin. He took our penalty as the perfect one who absorbed the judgment for our broken and sinful world. Then Jesus rose from the dead showing His power as God over all creation.

"Behold," Jesus says in Revelation 21:5, "I am making all things new" (ESV). A day is coming in Christ when we won't have to battle sin. Our hearts, minds, bodies, and desires will be made whole, never to be broken again.

One day Jesus will give us rescued bodies and minds, but today He offers us rescued hearts. In Ezekiel 36:26–28 God says, "I will give you a new heart, and a new spirit I will put within you ... I will put my Spirit within you and cause you to walk in my statutes and be careful to obey my rules ... and you shall be my people, and I will be your God" (ESV).

Except for people with gender dysphoria? Except for the young man or woman who is fighting lust? Except for the same-sex attracted person? No! The Bible says restoration is fully available to any and all through the good news of Jesus Christ that we call the gospel.

What does sexual restoration look like on a day-to-day basis this side of heaven? How does God work out sexual purity in our lives while we are still living in a broken world? Instead of removing every temptation toward sin, God promises He will be with us *through* every temptation and empower us to walk in holiness for His glory and our joy.

As any follower of Christ can attest, if someone struggles with lust, after he or she comes to Christ, God doesn't cause every good-looking person to disappear. The Internet doesn't just break. They're not immediately unsubscribed from every e-mail list. After someone puts on a wedding ring, everyone other than their spouse doesn't cease to be attractive. But the person's *want to* is changed. God's right authority and kingship are recognized. The person's way is aligned toward the right goal, and joyfully they say, *Whatever I have been given, I will trust and surrender it to Christ.*

Though we are still sexually broken, and our inclinations may be toward a variety of *porneia*, our ultimate desire is changed. We see that God is right, and we trust that He is good. We care more about God's glory than following our feelings. We see that God's ways truly lead to life. God calls each of us to something better than sex. God calls us to holy sexuality.

God has clearly defined what gender, sex, sexuality, and marriage are, and He never gave up His authority over these things. The question is whether we will try to take them from His hands or instead surrender to His will, finding joyful obedience in walking in God's ways in all our lives, including our sexuality.

So how can we help our friends, families, church members, and neighbors who are having "casual" sex, experience same-sex attraction, or have gender dysphoria? We will focus on that in the next chapter. Just as we are called to sexual holiness, we are called to love our neighbors, even those whose struggle with sin is different from ours.

QUESTIONS FOR FURTHER STUDY AND REFLECTION

1. What is something you learned from this chapter?
2. How did you respond to the idea that we are all outside the circle?
3. How did Jesus treat people who were sexually broken? Why did He treat them that way?
4. Do you believe that God is right and His definitions are good? How do you see that reflected in your life?
5. How are you going to apply what you learned in this chapter?

PART 8

LOVINGLY ENGAGING OUR FRIENDS AND NEIGHBORS WITH TRUTH

An Unfortunate Acknowledgment

Something needs to be acknowledged up front. If you turn on the TV or open social media, Bible-believing Christians and people engaged in our sexualized culture seem to be at polarized odds with each other. This is especially true when it comes to our LGBTQA+ neighbors.

Christians are often portrayed in the media as looking down on the LGBTQA+ community as if those in that group are beneath them. Sexually promiscuous people in movies and on TV seem to be having all the fun, while Christians stand from afar and point judgmental fingers.

To say that you're a Christian in many settings today will immediately have you labeled as an intolerant bigot. By the same token, to say you're pro-LGBTQA+ will often have you labeled as a flaming liberal. In virtually every voice of the media, the combination of Christianity, sexual promiscuity, and the

LGBTQA+ community seems to be like the combination of fire, gasoline, and dynamite.

In reality, most people I know who are truly trying to follow Christ have a sincere desire to love the LGBTQA+ community and, in a heartbeat, would buy them coffee, read the Bible with them, and gladly listen to them detail their journey. Most Christians I know are just very inexperienced with the LGBTQA+ community and don't know how to approach their neighbors or family members without fear of damaging a relationship or making something worse for the other person. They just don't want to cause an explosion and hurt somebody.

Many same-sex attracted, gender dysphoric, self-identifying LGBTQA+, or sexually promiscuous people are open to Jesus. They are interested in the Bible. However, they would be very nervous about walking through the doors of any local church because what they've been told is that Christians hate them. They've been told that God hates them, that the Bible tells us to hate them, and that there is no place for them in the church. The perception for them is that engaging with a Christian or walking through the doors of a church would be like stepping on a land mine.

People from all perspectives seem stuck in a narrative that I honestly believe mostly exists on the fringes of our social reality. But the voices are so loud and the headlines are so in our face that it seems like we are in the middle of a heated war against one another. There is a huge perceived gap: Christians on one side, LGBTQA+ advocates on the other side. Both sides seem to be lobbing labels and mean words because they're too afraid to enter the gap, engage with each other, and actually talk with or listen to each other. We are afraid the gap is full of land mines.

The problem with that approach for followers of Christ is that Jesus didn't do gaps. Jesus wasn't satisfied with the "us"-over-here-and-"them"-over-there mentality. He went *to* the woman at the well who was using sex loosely and repeatedly destroying the marriage covenant. Jesus defended the woman caught in adultery; not her adultery itself, but her as a person made in the image of God. God sent Philip to share the gospel with the confused eunuch from another country. In fact, the only reason any of us can have any hope at all is that God Himself, though infinitely holy and pure, crossed over the gap and came to be one of us. He willingly jumped on our land mine so that we could have a clear way back to Him. Then He rose from the grave so that sinners of every letter could be raised to life with Him.

How do we love our LGBTQA+ or sexually promiscuous neighbors? The way that Jesus loved us. We must enter the gap. But let's be honest: this kind of love is complicated. It is often very messy and requires much wisdom. Every situation is as unique as every person is unique.

What I cannot offer you are "Three Quick and Easy Steps to Fix Your LGBTQA+ or Sexually Promiscuous Neighbor"! That's not what it's about. This discussion is not about *steps* to *fix them*. It's about Jesus, the only person who truly heals any and all of us. While others said, "You can't go there! There's a gap between us and them," Jesus willingly and joyfully walked into that gap with truth and hope in the gospel. So how can we do the same?

Start with Yourself

Examine yourself first. Consider whether your view of God aligns with what the Bible says. Admit that there are areas of your life, sexual and otherwise, where you are not trusting and following Jesus. If you are a Christ follower, examine whether you are treating those whose sexual sin is different from yours as unworthy of the same salvation Christ brought to you.

Do you view others as important to God, made in His image, and worthy of love, compassion, respect, and truth? How is this reflected in your life? There may be areas of your life where you need to, in Jesus's words, take the wooden beam out of your own eye before you try to take the splinter out of someone else's eye (Matthew 7:4–5).

Equip Yourself with Truth

First and foremost, Christians must know the truth, not just statistics about the truth. While numbers and figures can provide scientific and medical arguments, issues of gender and sexuality go much deeper than data. Ultimately, your disagreement with someone of a different perspective isn't rooted in arguments but worldviews. The battle is really between the authority of God and the authority of man.

If we are going to engage a broken world, we must be equipped with the truth. Jesus Himself said He is the truth in John 14:6. Jesus calls sinners not only to follow the truth in obedience but also to know Him by following His word on the path of righteousness. As Jesus proclaimed to His followers, "If you abide in my word, you are truly my disciples, and you will know the truth, and the truth will set you free" (John 8:31–32 ESV).

Paul likewise tells his disciple Timothy, "Do your best to present yourself to God as one approved, a worker who has no need to be ashamed, rightly handling the word of truth" (2 Timothy 2:15 ESV).

When we aren't fully confident in what we believe or are pushed further on an idea than we have been before, our natural posture becomes that of defense. If we don't feel equipped with adequate knowledge, we will often try to arm ourselves with worldly weapons. When that happens, rather than seeing the person we are engaging as someone to love, we see them as an opponent to conquer. We go from trying to win them to trying to beat them.

You can't engage someone with love if your posture toward them is hostile. If we are confident in the faith, having equipped ourselves with the truth found in the Scriptures, we are much better suited to engage someone in conversation. We are more comfortable listening to someone detail their story and asking follow-up questions if we aren't always looking for an edge to make ourselves look smart. As Paul states, "The Lord's servant must not be quarrelsome but kind to everyone, able to teach, patiently enduring evil, correcting his opponents with gentleness. God may perhaps grant them repentance leading to a knowledge of the truth, and they may come to their senses and escape from the snare of the devil, after being captured by him to do his will" (2 Timothy 2:24–26 ESV).

Christians must not only know the truth, but they must also share the truth. It's been said that the gospel came to you on its way to someone else.[31] Christians must share the good news of the gospel with others just as God used others to explain and extend His mercy to them.

Paul warns Christians by reminding them that they are not to remove themselves from the sexually immoral people in the world but to be actively involved in helping them be set free by the truth. "I wrote to you in my letter," Paul explains, "not to associate with sexually immoral people—not at all meaning the sexually immoral of this world, or the greedy and swindlers, or idolaters, since then you would need to go out of the world" (1 Corinthians 5:9–10 ESV).

Paul perhaps recalled Jesus's prayer on behalf of His disciples recorded in John 17:15–18: "I do not ask that you take them out of the world, but that you keep them from the evil one. They are not of the world, just as I am not of the world. Sanctify them in the truth; your word is truth. As you sent me into the world, so I have sent them" (ESV).

---

[31] Robby Gallaty, *Growing Up: How to Be a Disciple Who Makes Disciples.* (Nashville, TN: B&H Publishing, 2013).

Thomas Schreiner observes, "Believers should 'show mercy' even to those deeply ensnared in sin. They were not to despise them or abhor those so defiled by sin. And yet their mercy should be mingled with fear and hatred, knowing that sin had stained and defiled these people in a remarkable way."[32]

The mission to glorify God includes the mission to tell of His glory to others. Romans 10:13–15 (ESV) captures this well: "For 'everyone who calls on the name of the Lord will be saved.' How then will they call on him in whom they have not believed? And how are they to believe in him of whom they have never heard? And how are they to hear without someone preaching? And how are they to preach unless they are sent? As it is written, 'How beautiful are the feet of those who preach the good news!'"

A person who is flirting with false teaching or listening to the siren call of sexual immorality must not be left by their Christian friends to fall into that trap. Instead, in Gene Green's words, "They must have him to coffee and chat it over with him in love. And they must know the faith so well that they can convince him while he is still hesitating … Such rescue work can never be done in any spirit of sanctimoniousness or superiority. It must be done in fear, in recognition that 'there, but for the grace of God, go I.'"[33] Christians must know and share the truth.

While Christians must know and share the truth, they must also always be mindful of the fact that they are not Jesus. Individually, Christians are incapable of crafting the perfect convincing argument or modeling the strictest holiness to save anyone.

Christians are also not the Holy Spirit. No amount of winsomeness, strategy, or friendliness can change someone else's heart. We must recognize that while we may be fleeing from sin,

---

[32]   Thomas R. Schreiner, *2 Peter, Jude*, Vol. 37, The New American Commentary (Nashville: B&H Publishing, 2003), 488–489.

[33]   Gene Green, *Jude and 2 Peter*, Baker Exegetical Commentary on the New Testament (Grand Rapids: Baker Academic, 2008), 212.

our enemy still lurks at our door seeking to devour us in a time of weakness. Christians must exercise discernment in sharing the truth. Echoing words from the book of Jude, Thom Schreiner states, "Believers are to beware lest their mercy is transposed into acceptance, and they themselves become defiled by the sin of those they are trying to help."[34] Even the most unrestrained heretic is not beyond the reach of God. Yet even the most committed Christian is not beyond the reach of sin.

So is the Christian to abandon those who are closest to the fire so they can save their own skin? Absolutely not. To remove ourselves from temptation, we must also take up the most significant weapon we have in the battle against sin: prayer to God on behalf of others. We must pray through the Spirit that God Himself will do the work that we cannot.

However, prayer is never to be considered a last resort. Prayer must be the first line of defense, the power that sustains through the battle, and the roar of final victory as God confronts sin and changes the sinner's heart. If we must leave a relationship or avoid a situation for a reasonable fear of being drawn into sin, we must remember the Holy Spirit's power to work in and through prayer. Prayer is the resource always available to the Christian when their presence is not.

Engage the Gaps

Our only hope in life and death is the good news, the gospel, of Jesus Christ. If you are a Christ follower, you know and experience this truth. You have God's word. You are fully equipped to engage a world full of sexual brokenness. Even if you don't know the answers to questions about sexuality, you do know the answer in the person of Jesus Christ. Share Him in truth and love.

---

[34]   Schreiner, *2 Peter, Jude,* 489.

As Christ followers, we must be willing to ask questions of ourselves and our LGBTQA+ neighbors. While not agreeing with all the assertions of LGBTQA+ activists or sexual progressives, we may need to engage channels of dialogue previously unopened.

Followers of Christ historically have been surprised at where Jesus's footsteps have led them or, more accurately, whom they have led them to. Jesus's disciples often found themselves in the homes of thieves, in the company of prostitutes, and in conversations with those they considered beneath their attention. Why? Because that's where Jesus went, with truth and hope in the gospel. Followers of Christ must be willing to do the same.

QUESTIONS FOR FURTHER STUDY AND REFLECTION

1. What is something you learned from this chapter?
2. How have you treated LGBTQA+ or sexually promiscuous people? What does Jesus think about the way you treat them?
3. What are some ways in Scripture that Jesus engaged gaps?
4. How are you equipping yourself with the truth? How could you do that more?
5. How are you going to apply what you learned in this chapter?

PART 9

SEX AND THE LOCAL CHURCH

The Helping Church

Real people. Real circumstances. Real feelings. Real prayers.

That's what I see more and more as I read the Scriptures: real people struggling to understand and trust a holy God. I see real circumstances in which people try to navigate a broken and sin-soaked world. I hear real prayers of those turning to God for truth and hope.

Imagine a person who gathers each week with your church family. He is experiencing thoughts and feelings he doesn't know what to do with. He doesn't see himself neatly fitting the gender stereotypes placed before him. He is confused and praying to God about what all this means. Would he know how to engage you or your church family with these questions?

Imagine a person walking through your church's doors for the first time. She's been invited by a friend but isn't sure what to expect. She has walls built up and has heard that Christians don't like people like her. She's heard God doesn't like people like her.

She is afraid, perhaps defensive. Would she be welcome to engage with you or your church family?

The church can easily feel ill-equipped, unprepared, and unsure about how to handle our society's broad acceptance of and encouragement toward a sexually broken and exploring world. How well is your church prepared?

The church has often been at arm's length from those who define their identity in sexual terms. But are these people at arm's length from the gospel? If not, how then should the church respond to our continually evolving sexual moment?

First, the church must understand the moment and its definitions. Second, the church must understand what it believes about human sexuality, why it matters, and what the Bible openly discusses in relation to male/female realities. The church must also recognize that there are those within our fellowship who find themselves wrestling with the fact that their feelings or experiences and the gender models placed before them do not line up. They are filled with questions and need an outlet for discussion. Where will they go to have this conversation? Our world has already created the dialogue and has its own answers that lead to a community with open arms. What will they find in the church?

To be clear, the church must not embrace the sexual revolution, but we may need to consider the way we embrace sexually deviant people. The blood of Christ does not stop at a levee of sexuality. While we must not give our affirmation, we need to be conversant with the issues of our day to give the gospel. We must know and speak the truth but do so in love as those who like everyone else have no hope apart from Jesus Christ.

What our sexually divergent neighbors need is the same thing the pastor, the liar, the small group leader, the addict, and the suburban soccer mom need: the gospel of Jesus Christ. LGBTQA+ people don't need a different gospel. Our sexually promiscuous friends and neighbors don't have a different Savior.

Like all of us in a broken and fallen world, they need to turn from the kingdom of self, surrender to Christ as King, and trust Him daily in new resurrected life.

The good news for the church is that we know the gospel. We have the Bible. We may not have a lot of training or a gender-studies degree from Harvard, but we can introduce people to Jesus.

Could it be difficult walking through the Bible, wrestling with big questions, and sharing the love of Jesus with a transgender neighbor? Absolutely. Frankly, it's hard for me to walk through the Bible, wrestle with big questions, and share the love of Jesus with myself! Ease is not our gospel paradigm.

A hopefully helpful paradigm for our churches to adopt in engaging our neighbors is simply this: Be clear about the whole gospel. When we speak of creation, it's important we talk not only about God as Creator, but also about *what* He has created. In speaking of His creation, it is vital we not only address the noes or boundaries but also the yesses and what joy, protection, provision, and flourishing those boundaries provide.

The Church and Gender

To engage a sexually questioning culture, we must affirm and uphold God's design of male and female, but also ensure we are providing *biblical* definitions—not baptizing *cultural* definitions. It is true that a lot of men like sports, the outdoors, and the combination of meat with fire. There is nothing wrong with that. However, that is not biblical manhood.

We must be willing to ask: does our church have room for the man who doesn't like sports or the woman who does? Do we clearly define, emphasize, and celebrate the biblical man who faithfully takes the initiative in leading his home toward Christ, yet prefers an art brush to a rifle? Do our youth understand that what they enjoy does not define their gender, but can be used within their gender to create a wonderful spectrum of people that God calls and uses in obedience to Him?

The church must be the champion of God's gender definitions and uphold the roles of biblical manhood and womanhood, but not filter them through cultural lenses first. We must teach on difficult passages and champion those who follow Christ well in marriage as well as singleness. Does your church affirm and celebrate the single adult with the same enthusiasm that Paul celebrates them with in his first letter to the Corinthians?

The Church and the Whole Gospel

The God of Genesis 1 created the genders of Genesis 2, and they were broken in Genesis 3, where we live today. It is important that we emphasize all three parts of this story. We live in a world of distortion, particularly sexual distortion.

Even some of the most important people in Scripture displayed sexual brokenness. David committed adultery and let his eyes go where they shouldn't. Rahab was a prostitute. Judah slept with his daughter-in-law, whom he thought was a prostitute. Not to mention Noah, Solomon, and others.

One of the biggest questions for people who embrace sexually promiscuous or LGBTQA+ lifestyles is, "Why would God make me this way if it is wrong?" Upholding what God created in Genesis 1–2 reminds us of how we are *created*, but pointing toward Genesis 3 helps us remember how we are *broken*.

As the church, we must be those who embrace, sympathize, and empathize with all who are broken and come together with them under the cross of Christ. The phrase "It's OK not to be OK, but it's not OK to stay that way" must be the church's refrain as we all come to grips with our condition.

While we are all broken images, distortions of what we are meant to be, we must continually remind one another that the story doesn't end at Genesis 3 but calls us forward to Revelation 21–22 when all things are restored and made new. Our neighbors need to know that we are all tempted by desires that run contrary to the truth. It is not those desires but what we do with them that expresses who we are.

The Bible invites us to cast off our old way of life, lay down our desires at the feet of Jesus, and walk in resurrected obedience to Him. When we come to Christ, God doesn't remove us from the sinful world. He does enable us, however, to recognize this world is not our home. One day God will restore us and make all things new. We can all look forward to that day together.

The gospel extends hope, joy, family, and redemption beyond what often fits the definitions we are used to. We need to do the same.

The Truthful Church

There are thousands of books, strategies, and ideas about how churches grow. Many church-growth models focus on numbers, ministries, events, and other means of building up the body. These things aren't bad, but when I think about church growth, I can't help but think of Paul's words to the church in Ephesus: "Speaking the truth in love, we are to grow up in every way into him who is the head, into Christ" (Ephesians 4:15 ESV) "Speaking the truth in love"—this is an often-neglected model for church growth.

In large part, the church finds itself woefully behind in conversations about human sexuality. Unfortunately, as we have been carrying on a very discreet, if at all, conversation within the church about godly sexuality, a much louder and multilayered conversation has grown outside our doors.

If our churches are to grow in biblical commitment and gospel-effectiveness, we are going to have to address some difficult topics. We must speak the truth of the gospel but also do so in a way that loves the church, equips our families, and spreads the hope of Jesus Christ to our neighbors.

The first rule for any church desiring to speak the truth about sex, gender, and sexuality in love is simply to do it. The Bible has a lot to say about sex, gender, and sexuality. God has clearly defined His beautiful purpose and plan for men, women, and their relationships. The Bible is unapologetic about our broken nature and how that nature works itself out in every aspect of our lives. The Word of God is active in its reach to address communities and people ravaged by sexual brokenness.

How can your church be a welcoming place for discussions about sex, gender, and sexuality? Preach hard texts and uphold the gospel of Jesus Christ. Make the ground level at the foot of the cross and champion Jesus as our only hope in life and death.

As the Word is preached and topics about sexuality, brokenness, confusion, or idolatry are presented, we shouldn't think these topics are taboo or best left to discussions behind closed doors. As we address examples of sexual brokenness, we must also remember we are talking about real people in real circumstances with real prayers. How would we want someone to talk about or share the gospel with us if we were in their shoes?

If we're not talking about gender and sexuality in the church, the only voices our people are hearing regarding these topics are from those who are uninfluenced by the Word of God. If the church is to join the conversation about sexuality today, we must be proactive. We must also be courteous and respectful to those who are personally struggling or who know someone who is struggling with sexuality or gender identity. We must remind our churches that there is room at the cross for the sexually broken.

For parents or leaders of kids or youth, conversations about sexuality can be difficult to approach. We need to remember, however, that the discussion has already started. Our kids are growing up in a world sloped toward gender fluidity and sexual perversion. We are only now recognizing how sharply slanted that slope is.

When it comes to conversations with our kids about sex, gender, and sexuality, the best place to start is by simply asking questions. Having conversations with our kids or teens at their level is essential. But we must know what their level is. Parents are often surprised at what their kids have seen or heard regarding sex, gender, and sexuality. They are also surprised to know how open their kids and teenagers may be to discussing those issues.

As mentioned earlier, these are conversations that our kids are growing up with. These topics are not as unapproachable to them as they may seem to us. As parents and ministry leaders, we must continually reinforce to our kids that we are safe people to come to with difficult questions and that the Bible has answers.

There is much more to say regarding the church and our sexually evolving culture. At this point, one of the most significant hurdles for the church to overcome in speaking the truth in love about sex is the double-edged assumption in our society that there is no truth and the church does not love. We will need to show our neighbors that we are not enemies that must be debated with but broken people adopted by an amazing God who want others to know the life-altering salvation available only through Jesus Christ.

Rather than gearing up for a debate, the most effective tool we can use in talking about and with our neighbors is the Bible. Reading through books of the Bible together allows Scripture itself to address tough topics in context and enables us to prayerfully walk alongside those with questions. The Bible should also give us the humility to remember that we are not better than anyone. Aside from the gospel of Jesus Christ, we are all dead in our sin.

As we speak the truth, let us do so with the love of Christ that led Him to the sexually broken woman at the well and called her to worship God in Spirit and truth. Let us be honest with one another in the way David was approached about and repented of his sexual brokenness. Let us be filled with the Spirit who guided Philip to the sexually-altered eunuch and led Paul to speak openly with the church of Corinth about the sexual confusion and distortions of their culture.

May we speak the truth in love and, in so doing, strengthen and grow the church under the authority and leadership of the One who is making all things new in Christ, including us.

QUESTIONS FOR FURTHER STUDY AND REFLECTION

1. What is something you learned from this chapter?
2. How has your church treated the issues of sex and sexuality?
3. How would an LGBTQA+ or sexually promiscuous person feel about coming to your church?
4. How can your church be more open with each other in talking about sex and sexuality?
5. How are you going to apply what you learned in this chapter?

PART 10
CONCLUSION

I want to thank you again for taking the time to read this book. While paper and ink can only express so much, I pray that the full heart of the gospel and God's desire to see us flourish within His design for sex, gender, and sexuality is apparent. No matter who you are or what conclusions you have come to, thank you for walking through this book with me.

Before you go, I want to introduce you to someone. This person is my friend. His story is not recorded in the Scriptures. He was a member of our church. He served with us, went to small groups with us, sang with us, opened God's Word, and took communion with us.

The first time I met this person formally was at a coffee shop. We sat down over steaming cups of hot caffeinated bean water and got to know each other. The usual topics of conversation were covered: family, background, questions about the church, etc.— the normal "get to know you" stuff.

Midway through the conversation, however, this person somewhat nervously disclosed to me that he was same-sex attracted. He said that he knew what God's Word said, he knew what the circle of God's design and protection was and that he was trusting the circle in his life. His big question was, even though he was trusting

God's design, given that he struggled with same-sex attraction, was there still a place for him in our church or was there a gap?

I listened to him and thanked him for his openness and honesty. I told him I was honored that he had trusted me with this information. I knew that was a difficult thing to do. Then I told him gladly and confidently that, yes, there was a place for him. "You'll fit right in," I said. "We're all broken sinners in need of a Savior who are trying to trust and follow Jesus together. Follow Him with us! You may be sexually broken in a different way than I am, but the church is a place for broken people to glorify God *together* by trusting Jesus *together*, fleeing sin *together*, and joyfully obeying all Jesus commands *together*."

This person moved away from our town several years later. We stayed in touch a bit here and there, but we really had not talked until one day I reached out to him on social media. I had been working on resources about God's design for sex, gender, and sexuality. I sent these resources to him and asked how someone from his perspective would interact with these tools. I asked if they were useful, helpful, compassionate, and charitable toward all kinds of readers. Shortly thereafter, he responded that the resources looked good and thanked me for sending them. The conversation concluded there.

Several months later, I woke up to an alert on my phone. The screen notified me that I had received a message from this person. I was excited and somewhat curious to see that he had sent me a long message. With his permission, I share it with you:

> *Hey Ryan! I just wanted to reach out and say thank you again for sending me the [resources]. Receiving [them] set off a series of chain reactions that led me back to a walk with the Lord. [About a year ago], I had really started to become entangled in sin in my life, specifically sin in the area of homosexuality.*

It started off innocent enough. However, by the time you messaged me, I was up to my eyeballs in sin. The whole time, I knew the Lord wanted better for me and wanted me to walk in truth in word and deed; however, I just didn't know how to get out or if I wanted to. I wanted so desperately to be able to live in that lifestyle and have a walk with Christ and there were many "Christians" claiming that such a life can be. I was beginning to believe that lie even though I could feel the Holy Spirit moving in my heart telling me otherwise.

The Lord used [the resources you sent] in an extremely powerful way in my life. A few weeks later I had a complete, full-on meltdown at 1:30 in the morning about what I was doing with my life, why I was running from the Lord, and how I had let myself get there.

The journey over the last several months has been incredibly hard. I was in such bondage to sin that it felt like I couldn't even approach the throne.

Jesus met me in my mess.

He grabbed my hands and started lifting me out of the pit I was in. I left the affirming church I was at and sought to find a Bible-believing church. I got connected to a solid local church, went to one of their young adult small groups, and got plugged in. I also began trying to have a daily quiet time with the Lord. It was a major struggle at first. I would make excuses as to why I couldn't get around to it. Mainly that I was too tired.

> *However, I began to pray that the Lord would give me a desire to pursue Him and spend time in His Word. Did He ever deliver. I made the decision that I was going to get up extra early and start my day with a time of Bible study before I left for work. It's been a game-changer. I've seen the Lord working in powerful ways in my life: changing my desires from wanting to pursue sin, to wanting to pursue Him.*

> *I have a long way to go on my journey. But the Lord has and continues to create a new heart in me. Sorry for such a long message. God has just been so faithful to me, and I'm just overwhelmed by His love and mercy. I wanted you to know that had you not sent that message, I don't know how long I would have stayed pursuing sin instead of righteousness. Thank you for being faithful to the Lord.*

This is not a story about anything I did or any resources I gave. I just gave him resources that tell the truth about biblical sexuality and have testimonies of people who are trusting God's design. The resources were not what made the difference. But notice what did: the faithful work of the Holy Spirit using the Word of truth in the context of local church relationships.

While the Spirit started something within him in a particular moment, it is not that emotional experience that is sustaining him. What is sustaining him? A Bible-believing church, a small group, daily prayer, and intentional Bible reading.

It's not magic. What's helping him is the work of God in and through a local church that is willing to walk with the sexually broken and tell the truth expressed in God's Word. That has been God's plan from the beginning, and it is still His plan today. The question for us is whether we will be that kind of people. Will we be that kind of church?

I would much rather use the church to serve myself. I would prefer to sit comfortably with my friends and family, talk with people I know and like, praise Jesus for what He's done for me, then go home and do it all again the next week. But if we are to be the church that God designed us to be, we must be willing to ask some honest questions of ourselves.

Do we really believe that sharing the truth, reading the Bible, being in community, and truly being the church with one another are tools that the Spirit still uses? Do we believe they are still strong enough for our neighbors in the midst of a sexually saturated culture that celebrates life outside of God's circle? Do we really believe that Jesus is better? Do we really believe that Jesus is the only way, the only truth, and the only life for our LGBTQA+ and sexually promiscuous neighbors? If so, we must be willing to enter the gap for them with truth, love, and compassion—the same way others have done for us.

QUESTIONS FOR FURTHER STUDY AND REFLECTION

1. What is something you learned from this book?
2. How has your understanding of sex and sexuality changed by reading this book?
3. How has your understanding of God and the Bible changed by reading this book?
4. Are you trusting the circle?
5. How are you going to apply what you learned in this book?
6. Who is someone in your life who needs to hear what is written in this book? How are you going to share it with them?

Afterword

How Did We Get Here, and Where Are We Going?

Shaping a Sexual Revolution

Several times in this book, I have mentioned a "sexual revolution" or spoken of the modern realities we encounter in relation to LGBTQA+ and sexually promiscuous lifestyles. Where has this sexual revolution come from? Unless we understand our history, we are doomed to repeat it.

While painting the historical backdrop for everything else in this book was beyond the purview and focus of the work, I believe it is important to at least give a brief synopsis of how we have landed in the cultural waters in which we find ourselves swimming.

What we see today in our culture are the continuously evolving applications of certain ideas which have come to be known as a sexual revolution. The use of the term *revolution* is appropriate in more ways than one. As many have noted, what we face today is not merely an incremental shift but a complete redefinition of core social and religious principles.

Albert Mohler observes, "We are facing a complete transformation of the way human beings relate to one another in the most intimate contexts of life. We are facing nothing less than a comprehensive redefinition of life, love, liberty, and the very meaning of right and wrong."[35]

While we could trace a variety of winds from which this storm has developed, and ultimately, we know the sexual revolution began with the fall of man in Genesis 3, it is helpful to note the pivotal adoption of certain sexual ideas under the wing of the scientific community in the early 1900s.

The first several years of the twentieth century introduced the scientific research of Sigmund Freud.[36] Freud was obsessed not only with sexuality but also with sexuality as a behavioral *instinct*. Following in the steps of Charles Darwin, Freud suggested that sexuality was a necessary and essential survival instinct at the core of our physical, emotional, and relational being. To Freud, sex was just a part of natural physical development and was a transactional act between two people. It was certainly not covenantal. The idea of sexuality being brought under the authority of a sovereign Creator God was not only repressive in Freud's view but also harmful to human flourishing. For Freud and those who were like-minded to him, sex was merely a biological function to be carried out personally as desired.

In 1918, the introduction of prophylactics (condoms, pills, etc.) to America separated sex from its natural relationship to family, procreation, and commitment between sexual partners. Once sex was rebranded as simply a bodily function driven by animal instinct without cords of responsibility, sex began to be seen as a personal product or service.

In 1948, Alfred Kinsey began studying a variety of sexual deviances. It should be noted that Kinsey was a pedophile who performed sexual experiments on children without their consent

---

[35]   Albert Mohler, *We Cannot Be Silent: Speaking Truth to a Culture Redefining Sex, Marriage, & the Very Meaning of Right & Wrong* (Nashville: Thomas Nelson, 2015), 1.

[36]   See Freud, Sigmund, *Three Essays on the Theory of Sexuality.* (Mansfield Centre, Connecticut: Martino Publishing, 2011).

even before their first birthday. In line with Freud's ideas, Kinsey sought to tear sexuality from the realm of objectivity and bring it into the light of celebrated subjectivity. To do so, Kinsey and his associates began peeling back layers of definition and accountability to accommodate sexual divergences' move to normalcy. Kinsey wrote his view as the following:

> Males do not represent two discrete populations, heterosexual and homosexual. The world is not to be divided into sheep and goats. Not all things are black nor all things white. It is a fundamental of taxonomy that nature rarely deals with discrete categories. Only the human mind invents categories and tries to force facts into separated pigeon-holes ... The sooner we learn this concerning human sexual behavior the sooner we shall reach a sound understanding of the realities of sex.[37]

The break-neck speed at which these ideas were adopted and applied is a sociological phenomenon. In 1953, Hugh Hefner introduced the first edition of *Playboy* magazine, tapping into a growing market for individual sexual gratification outside the marital covenant. Urbanization, technological advances, and changes in sexual laws all promoted the twentieth-century ideas of sexual "freedom."

Fast forward to the 1990s—as Fulbright Scholar Carmine Sarracino and Albany State University professor Kevin M. Scott observed, "By the 1990s, not only had children become thoroughly sexualized in movies, advertisements, and marketing,

---

[37] Alfred C. Kinsey, Wardell B. Pomeroy, and Clyde E. Martin, *Sexual Behavior in the Human Male* (Indianapolis: Indiana University Press, 1948), 177.

but something more general had begun to occur: the sexualization of just about everyone, regardless of age or status in society."[38]

By the end of the decade, as Albert Mohler notes, "Most respected mainstream academic institutions in America featured academic departments that were devoted entirely to the study and promotion of the strangest and most exotic theories of human sexuality—and often their practice as well."[39]

Previously unchallenged categories of male and female were blending into a sexual spectrum in which one's sexual drive and appetite determined one's "identity."

Homosexuality was becoming normative in culture as well as law, and any appeal to an objective authority over sex and sexuality was not only mocked but also vilified. Virtually everyone under the age of thirty today has been born into a world in which biblically-opposed ideas about sex are mainstream. They have been swaddled in a cultural revolution primed to indoctrinate them into the new cultural norms.

The cultural conversation has been going on for decades. The discussion in the church is still relatively young. Though present in virtually every letter of the New Testament, we must consider whether the presence of such open dialogue concerning sexuality is equally present in the sermons, small groups, and coffee-shop conversations of our local churches.

An assumption has long held sway that if we tell students to avoid sex and give them doctrinally vague answers to a few questions about sexuality, they will embrace a thorough sexual ethic and will not ask awkward questions. This idea is proving to be inaccurate. Unfortunately, this practice has been dominant in recent history and has greatly shaped today's Christian young adults.

---

[38]   Carmine Sarracino and Kevin M. Scott, *The Porning of America: The Rise of Porn Culture, What It Means, and Where We Go from Here* (Boston: Beacon Press, 2008), 29.

[39]   Mohler, *We Cannot Be Silent*, 13.

Another item of note is that it was not until the latter decades of the twentieth century and into the twenty-first, that the church began offering significant publications on sex and sexuality. However, these offerings were decades behind the already cemented ethos of the sexual revolution. In an attempt to regain footing, such resources gave quick biblical answers about sex and purity but did not provide a robust biblical apologetic as to why holy sexuality is necessary for God's glory as well as the good of individuals and society.

Such writings were also not widely distributed among young Christians and did not adequately address common misunderstandings about biblical sexuality.

Thankfully, in recent years, the church has been responding with a variety of orthodox voices who are championing God's design for sex, gender, and sexuality. Conversations are opening and voices that may not have gained a hearing in the Christian conversation a few years ago are being brought to the fore.

It is my sincere hope and prayer that these discussions will continue to grow to the point that God's Word is a recognized and respected voice in the cultural discussion regarding sex, gender, and sexuality. I hope these discussions will grow in your own life and in your church. I also pray that in some small way, this writing may contribute to that reality for God's glory and the good of His people.